Love in Action

Published by Eagle, an imprint of Inter Publishing Service (IPS) Ltd, 59 Woodbridge
Road, Guildford, Surrey GU1 4RF.

Typeset by The Electronic Book Factory Ltd, Fife, Scotland
Printed in India.

ISBN No: 0 86347 107 2

Love in Action

Celebrating 25 years of Tear Fund

Melanie Symonds

EAGLE
GUILDFORD, SURREY

CONTENTS

Foreword by Cliff Richard   9
1   Help Behind the Headlines   11
2   In the Beginning   20
3   George Hoffman 1933–1992   34
4   Good News to the Poor   44
5   They Can't Eat Prayer   51
6   Bangladesh: Love Never Gives Up   63
7   Ethiopia: a Future and a Hope   74
8   The Philippines: Broken Image   81
9   India: a Heart for the Poor   89
10 Uganda: Compassion has the Heart   99
11 Brazil: Children on the Edge   108
12 Honduras: Whose Earth?   119
13 Tearcraft: a World of Creation   124
14 Women Like Us   130
15 Walk in His Shoes   138
16 Tear Fund Today   146
17 Love in Action   154

PHOTOGRAPHIC CREDITS

The author and publishers are grateful to the following for the use of their photographs, so kindly made available to illustrate this tribute to the work of Tear Fund.

Bruce, Richard – Tear Fund, p.93; Capon, John – Tear Fund, p.109; Collins, Rose – Tear Fund, p128; Greenleaf, pp21, 23, 32, 32, 37, 40, 60, 61, 66, 69, 69, 69, 72, 73, 77, 81, 83, 84, 85, 88, 97, 112, 113, 117, 121, 125, 129, 133, 141, 141, 141, 153; Jackson, Lorna – Tear Fund, p152; Loring, Jim – Tear Fund, pp9, 32, 45, 49, 100, 100, 104, 105, 107, 111, 149, 156; Page, Michael, p22; Reid, Andrew – Frank Spooner Pictures pp12; Relph, Penny – Tear Fund, pp13, 32; Smith, Leonard, p32; Tear Fund Archives, pp7, 28, 35, 47, 75, 90, 92; Verma, Santosh, p125; Webb, Mike – Tear Fund, pp4, 25, 44, 57, 78, 80, 87, 89, 89, 93, 96, 97, 97, 101, 102, 103, 108, 116, 120, 123, 125, 130, 132, 137, 139, 141, 154, 156; Wilson, Stephen – Tear Fund, pp16, 17.

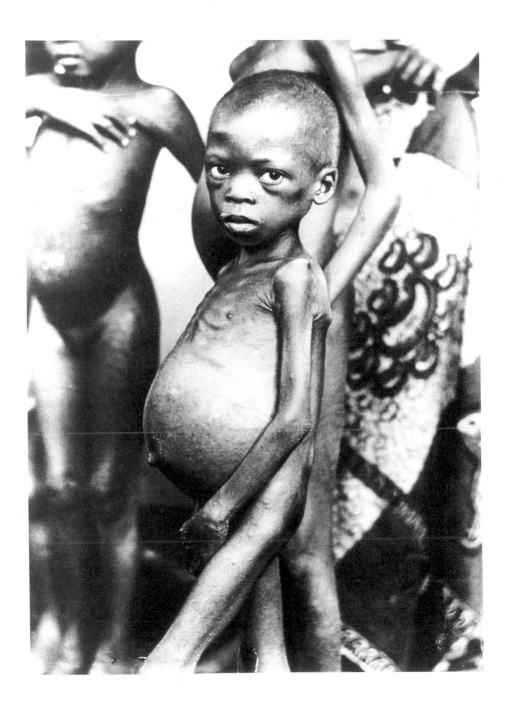

FOREWORD

The story has been well documented. When someone trod on that child's hand in a squalid Bangladesh refugee camp back in the early 1970s, my instinct was to pick him up and hold him. In that instant, the smell and the dirt and the babies' sores didn't matter, and I learned a lesson that profoundly altered my perspective and understanding. A Third World image, previously sanitised and kept at bay within TV news bulletins, became reality; a statistic became a person. Through what was to be an appeal for funds, I personally encountered an appeal for love, and I realised I was in a position to offer both. By virtue of my public platform and so-called 'celebrity status', I had a unique opportunity to communicate what I saw and experienced and, via songs and video, was able to prompt others to pray and to give; by virtue of my Christian faith, I understood my obligation to reflect not my feeble sympathy but God's practical compassion. 'To whom much is given', I read in Scripture, 'much is required, for greater is their responsibility.'

In all respects, identification and involvement with Tear Fund

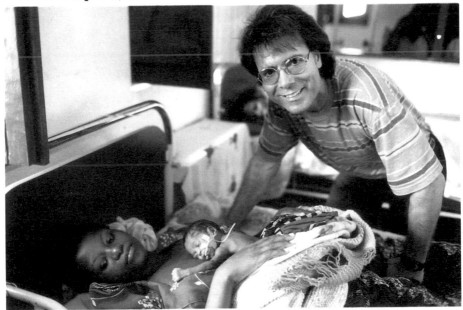

has been an enriching experience. I constantly feel that I receive far more than I give. I recall the privilege of meeting Christian nurses working in the back of beyond in Southern Sudan and being overwhelmed not only by their dedication but by their sheer courage and fantastic sense of humour, despite the potential loneliness and danger. There was the home of a long-serving missionary on the remote island of La Gonave, a few miles from Haiti, where the marvellous aroma of freshly-baked bread seemed so out of context. I remember walking with Salvation Army workers through alleys running with sewage in Haiti slums, and producing hilarious reactions from Maasai tribeswomen as I sang to them in the plains of Kenya. More recently I prayed with a lady dying of AIDS in a village in Uganda, and talked with Bishop Misaeri Kauma about the Church's efforts to combat and educate about the disease in urban Kampala.

My memories are various and vivid. On most trips I travelled with George Hoffman, Tear Fund's First Executive Director. His death in a road accident in England in 1992 was hard to accept – even harder to understand. For many years George had been a friend and encourager, and his commitment to the sad and hungry was an inspiration. 'We must hang on to the fact that God doesn't make mistakes,' said Franklin Graham at George's funeral. I have to believe he was right. The large framed photograph taken by George that hangs in my bedroom at home, showing me ashen-faced and being clasped like a koala bear by that Bangladeshi baby, now has even greater meaning and poignancy.

I recently ended another of my gospel concert tours, which raise funds for both Tear Fund and my own charitable trust. It was one of the happiest and most fruitful tours for some time, and to be able to share a little of Tear Fund's work and challenge with thousands of people from a concert stage was the best way I know to celebrate and to say 'thank you' for 25 remarkable years.

Cliff Richard

CHAPTER ONE

HELP BEHIND THE HEADLINES

Bosnia: the need

Should the West send in the troops? Would they get embroiled in another Vietnam?

While Britain and her NATO allies pondered the fate of the Balkans in 1993, there were other, pressing human needs, as the British newspapers revealed day by day. Grotesque 'ethnic cleansing' policies by both the Serbs and Croats had displaced thousands of people; incredibly, Europe, the continent which would consider itself the most advanced in the world, had a refugee problem in its midst. It also had a starvation problem, a shelter problem and a deep-rooted spiritual problem; that of man's inhumanity to man, as base in the twentieth century as in the first century AD.

A newscaster announced, 'At the moment we seem to be in a particularly bloody patch,' an accurate but naive statement to those about to recognise the 25th anniversary of Tear Fund. Since 1968 it has been helping to mop up the world's 'bloody patches', aware that empty stomachs and aching hearts have usually been in existence long before they reach the newspapers and television. But Tear Fund, true to its unique status as a relief and development organisation run by British and Irish evangelical Christians in partnership with evangelical Christians overseas, has been concerned to bring help to the whole person. Its carefully administered funds bring help – and *hope*. The hope may be in a brighter future for a family's children, or the fundamentally important assurance of peace with God and forgiveness of sins.

So it is not headlines which have dictated Tear Fund's agenda. It is poverty, injustice, and a very biblical concern to see the love of God literally spread abroad.

Tear Fund is more a support than a relief organisation. When disaster strikes, its expertise lies in enabling evangelical Christians on the spot to respond to the needs around them.

Having said this, its well-proven method of working with responsible Christian leaders overseas means that it is often able to receive news and needs of national disasters as they happen.

This is what happened in the former Yugoslavia, where its long-standing contact was able to appeal directly to his colleagues in Britain.

'We need food, clothes, medicines and toiletries,' announced publisher Dr Branko Lovrec of the publishing house Duhovna Stvarnost ('Christian Resource Centre') in Croatia.

Tear Fund promptly channelled financial support to this partner organisation which has liaised with local churches who provided volunteers and some finance. They provided for convoys of lorries to take food, clothing, medicines and blankets. The refugees themselves helped with distribution of food and medicines, thus living up to a vital Tear Fund policy of helping people to help themselves.

At the request of the government, Duhovna Stvarnost was providing food and hygiene items to 600 refugee families in the Croatian capital, Zagreb. Many had escaped from the war zones of Bosnia with no personal belongings; now they were living in warehouses and sports halls. The government had also given the organisation a new distribution centre in the southern Croatian port of Dubrovnik, so they were even able to send food and medicine directly to several towns in war-torn Bosnia-Herzegovina, often to places where the United Nations had been refused access.

The need on the doorstep

As Duhovna Stvarnost was not a relief organisation, simply a concerned Christian Publisher who saw the need on their doorstep, Tear Fund sent out one of its consultants, Richard Reynolds, to advise them.

Much of the food came from churches in the West as one-off

A woman surveys what remains of her neighbourhood in Vitez

donations. More regular assistance came from relief and development agencies like Tear Fund, who contributed £100,000 for the purchase of local food. It was cheaper to buy food at the rate of 150 tons per month from Hungary and Austria than to load lorries in England.

'Providing food for people in Bosnia keeps them there,' Richard explained. 'If they left their homes, they'd never return, but would enter Western Europe as refugees.'

Tear Fund's money was mainly used for soup kitchens, served from lorries, with the aim of giving everyone a daily main meal of hearty soup and bread. 'People would bring a big pot and collect soup for their family,' said Richard. 'That way it kept people's dignity because they could take it back and eat at home.'

Richard went to Dubrovnik, whose population had been swollen by immigrants from the burnt and looted surrounding towns. With the tourist trade just a memory, the hotels were now full of displaced people.

In Zagreb, Duhovna Stvarnost arranged its distribution from an office in the main square. In this and other places under fire, work carried on despite the room being shaken by shellfire every 30 seconds.

Richard found that his Yugoslavian colleagues valued Tear Fund's willingness to operate at their pace and unwillingness to control their operation.

With everyone working all hours, Richard spent time checking through administrative procedures, the organisation's administrative set-up, now that its computers, which previously contained Bible notes, were employed to list medicines and other supplies stored in the warehouse. 'Receiving convoys of goods from the West is extremely complicated,' explains Jennie Evans of Tear Fund's Overseas Department. 'You have to log them in, making sure everything is of suitable quality, then decide how best to distribute and transport them.'

Since the evangelical church in the former Yugoslavia was very small, Tear Fund's partners found they could work with both the Catholics and Muslims without being seen to be partisan.

But Duhovna Stvarnost stickers on boxes ensure recipients always know the aid comes from Christians. 'When the trucks come, people visit the office in Zagreb and talk to Ivan, a Duhovna Stvarnost worker,' reported Richard.

And they take extra care because it's their own people. They ask what the people want – they're not given just any box – because they may want nappies, soap or coffee. It's so easy to dehumanise aid.

I saw three girls in their early 20s, formerly students of economics, looking after a soup kitchen. It was hot and smoky in there and there was shelling in the background. Next day Ivan packed three boxes of toiletries specially for those girls and personally delivered them.

Hope in a hopeless situation

Branko and his colleagues did not forget their first love. Distribution of Bible notes went on alongside food distribution, including a book by Billy Graham, *Peace with God*, and a book by Cliff Richard, translated into Serbo-Croat.

In Croatia, Duhovna Stvarnost had good relations with the small but strong Catholic Church there and had given 15,000 copies of the Bible notes *Daily Bread* to Catholic priests. The success of their operation with only eight full-time staff could be partly measured by their meeting with a priest in the burnt-out shell of a school at the other end of the country who cheerfully announced, 'I read your Bible notes.'

Ivan was talking to a Muslim imam in a leather jacket at their distribution point in Orasjia, who encouraged him by saying, 'You don't read your notes – it says today in *Daily Bread* not to give up!'

They left the imam holding a copy of a Billy Graham book and waving goodbye.

Tony Neeves, Tear Fund's former Communications Director, visited Croatia more than once during the war. He saw hardened soldiers on the front line who were 'tremendously pleased' to receive copies of these books, offering hope for the future in a hopeless situation. He met civilians who had had their farms, animals and homes destroyed, while some had seen their loved ones slaughtered. Leaving the ruins, they migrated to Zagreb. Tony met doctors, nurses, teachers and musicians, newly dressed in secondhand clothing from the British convoys, who expressed great joy at receiving Christian literature along with their clothes and food. He found it a very moving experience, because every time he went out there, the people said to him, 'We're amazed that people in England are concerned enough about what is happening to us to send clothes and food.'

Richard Reynolds sums up his findings of this operation; although unique in itself, like every Tear Fund operation, the active concern has been seen many times over the past 25 years: 'Working with Duhovna Stvarnost had been what I imagined Tear Fund was about – being wise with money and sensitive to people, especially in emergency situations.'

Partners in trouble

When disaster strikes, Christians are always ready to respond. Tear Fund's network of evangelical partners are on the spot, often able to assess and meet need with great speed and effectiveness.

Partner Portrait
Dr Branko Lovrec,
Duhovna Stvarnost, Croatia

Branko first worked with Tear Fund in the late 1960s becoming a close friend to George Hoffman. He had given up his medical practice to start publishing and distributing Christian literature under the Communist regime, with all the oppression that such a venture entailed. Through its long-time associate organisation, Eurovangelism, led by Dave Foster, Tear Fund was able to make grants to his work discreetly.

The pastor of a Baptist church in Zagreb, Branko has fluent English and has interpreted for Billy Graham during his crusades in the Balkans when the Communist era was over. According to Tony Neeves, who has worked with Branko over the years, he is a remarkable man. 'He's very dynamic – not a fit man – but one of the most godly men I've ever met, with great vision and determination to carry on his work of distributing Christian literature.'

Although Branko and his company already had vital work in hand, that of translating and distributing daily Bible notes and books, the tragedies around them caused them to add relief work to their publishing programme following the outbreak of fighting in 1991 when Serbia invaded Croatia.

'Branko's small team had been publishing literature for the past 15 years, but given the needs surrounding them, they felt they couldn't stand back, and had to become involved. So some of the team concentrated on relief work, while Branko and his wife carried on the publishing, although Branko still oversaw the relief work,' says Jennie Evans.

That inability to stand back and watch others suffer is the quality to be found not only in Branko Lovrec, but in all the partners with whom Tear Fund has been privileged to work over its 25 year history.

Tear Fund team fights famine in Mozambique

Tear Fund's story is one of partnership. As well as working with other nationals, it regularly teams up with other agencies to ensure the success of major projects.

In July 1992 it sent David de Leyser to lead a team of 12 Christians – logisticians, accountants and nutritionists – from different relief agencies to Mozambique, to help churches distribute food to refugees from rebel-held areas in the Limpopo River Valley.

The other workers came from World Relief and Christian Outreach. Together they set up food distribution centres in the Gaza province, southern Mozambique, where the people were suffering famine as a result of the second year of drought. The area was also threatened by the right-wing Renamo group who were fighting the formerly Marxist government, making it difficult to get urgent supplies through to the people in need.

With bandits making road travel dangerous, the team sometimes had to fly to the local churches administering the food to their communities. Air Serve, the relief arm of Mission Aviation Fellowship, USA, flew them in from their base camps.

As well as sending its skilled workers, Tear Fund sent £75,000 for food and water supplies in the stricken area. The famine affecting Southern Africa has been exacerbated in Mozambique by 15 years of civil war which only ended in 1992. The biggest need

David de Leyser, Mozambique Relief Project Director, visiting a village where food has been distributed.

was to provide infrastructure and logistical support to protect the supplies necessary for people's survival and future development; water, food and agricultural seeds and tools.

Mozambique's projected food requirement rose from 600,000 tons in May 1992 to 1.3 million tons a year later, due to the drought. In coalition with the other agencies, Tear Fund was able to deliver 9–10,000 tons of food between late October 1992 and the end of March 1993, as well as delivering seeds and tools to 22,000 farming families.

Water was a significant need, because the Limpopo River had almost dried up, so the team had to help displaced communities clustered in the country's 'railway corridor' for safety.

Kevin McKemey, who served with Tear Fund for many years and currently acts as consultant to World Relief, visited the area and was impressed by the efficiency of the operation devised by David:

> They experienced a *very* low loss rate. Mozambique is famous for materials going missing, but this team was effective; they did a good job of control and management which didn't allow loopholes. The lack of abuse was obvious to observers who'd experienced alternative types of distribution. This is due to Rob Stockdale of Tear Fund who handled the logistics and Phil Chester of Christian Outreach.

He was also impressed by the 'providential' way that water was discovered. Credit goes to Tear Fund water engineers Willie Hume and Steve Ray – and to the power of answered prayer. 'They hit a band of water 160 metres long and a few metres wide in an area where it was considered impossible to hit water. Now they're continuing to strike water in different communities, which has an enormous impact on a community's morale.'

An additional encouragement for Tear Fund supporters at home was the fact that the work was being carried out openly in the name of local evangelical churches, providing a Christian response to the crisis.

A striking use of black and white imagery and statistics have been a feature of Tear Fund's promotion. These two posters are part of a set produced in the early eighties.

SPIRITUAL RICHES

'We don't have all this world's goods and sometimes we get upset about it and we get cross that people have riches and we don't, that people are comfortable and we're not: that people are able to get medical care for their children, whereas we don't. But overall we know we have a place in heaven and we have a hope of being with the Lord one day and we see the rich and we see that for all they have they are not happy–they are not content. And so we thank God that we have a real hope for the future.'

A Chaco Indian, living in Northern Argentina

In the UK almost all homes have electricity and a piped water supply; 9 out of 10 families have a refrigerator; two-thirds of households have the use of a car. And yet, amidst all this prosperity, 1 in 3 marriages ends in divorce; the increasing number of abortions is over 100,000 each year; 25 million tranquillizers were prescribed in 1977; and each year fewer and fewer people attend a regular place of worship.

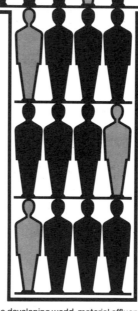

1 person in 4, in Africa, now attends a place of worship on a regular basis.

Almost all homes have water and electricity.

9 out of 10 families have a fridge.

2 out of 3 houses use a car.

1 in 3 marriages end in divorce.

100,000 abortions each year.

25 million tranquillizers were prescribed in 1977.

In the developing world, material affluence is often lacking but more and more people are coming to know the saving love of the Lord Jesus Christ.
In Africa, over 6 million people became Christians in 1978.
The population of Brazil is expanding at a rate of 2.8% per year, but the Protestant Church is growing 3 times faster.

"Life is more than food, and the body more than clothing."
Luke 12:23

POVERTY AND RICHES

Every child born in an industrialised country is likely to consume between 20 and 40 times as much of the world's resources as a child born in a developing country.

The United Nations have estimated that 1800 calories per day are the minimum requirement for a person to subsist, and 2300 are the minimum for a healthy life.

3345	2300	2000	1800
Britain Calories per day	Minimum (Heathly Life)	Developing Countries (Under 2000)	Minimum (needed to survive)

In India, Guatemala, Tanzania and many other developing countries the average consumption is less than 2000 calories per day, whereas in Britain the figure is 3345.

The average income in the UK is over £80 per week: 10 times higher than in the developing countries.

Official overseas aid sent to the developing countries by our government is equivalent to 26p per week per person and we give a further 1p per person through the voluntary agencies.

Proportion of population without access to safe water

Only 1 in 7 homes in the world enjoy a piped water supply and over a quarter of the world's population have no access to safe water.

92%	**Ethiopia**
89%	**Indonesia**
66%	**Bolivia**
44%	**Bangladesh**
NIL	**Western Europe**

"Give me neither poverty nor riches. Give me just enough to satisfy my needs. For if I grow rich, I may become content without God."
Proverbs 30:8,9

TEAR FUND

CHAPTER TWO

IN THE BEGINNING

'It never occurred to any of us that it would grow so much,' says former Tear Fund chairman Glyn Macaulay of the charity's extraordinary success.

Tear Fund was born 25 years ago in a committee room of the Evangelical Alliance in London. Since 1960, World Refugee Year, the Evangelical Alliance had been receiving gifts to help missionaries working with refugees. The donors clearly wanted their money to be used in an evangelical context.

To date the money had been used for the benefit of refugees in Hong Kong, channelled through the Rev Henry Donnithorne and his wife, Gladys, who had set up a work centre for refugees there. As far as Rev Gilbert Kirby, the Evangelical Alliance's General Secretary was concerned, they were making an evangelical contribution to World Refugee Year. But eight years later, the fund was still in existence, the recipient of a steady trickle of gifts, which it paid out to missionary societies at six-month intervals. The fund seemed necessary because of the continuing needs of refugees brought to their notice.

When Rev Morgan Derham succeeded Gilbert Kirby in 1966 as General Secretary of the Evangelical Alliance, he had an ambition for the fund; he wanted to set up a full-scale relief and development fund. By that time other aid agencies had been established, but evangelical Christians were not always prepared to support them because they were regarded as either too 'secular' or too 'liberal' in their theology: they did not seem to be committed to sharing the gospel.

'My intention was to remove that alibi and set up a fund to which no evangelicals could take exception, and at the same time educate the evangelical constituency into taking social responsibilities seriously.'

Having had his brainchild approved by the EA Council, Morgan appointed a young graduate from the London School of Economics to carry out research for the new fund. Mary-Jean Duffield, already believing God would somehow use her to help those threatened by the 1966 famine in Bihar, brought political enthusiasm to her work.

I read a lot about Oxfam, Christian Aid and the Ministry of

Defence, who were all very co-operative, and helped Morgan run a couple of London house groups where we discussed our ideas. But I can't tell you how small our work was then – the fund office consisted of one desk in a corner.

Nonetheless, by the time George Hoffman arrived to take on a daunting amount of work, the relief fund file, just one of twelve for which he was given responsibility, was, thanks to Mary-Jean's efforts, quite substantial. Mary-Jean was invited to join the first EAR Fund committee. 'The fund grew of itself – it was as if it had a life of its own,' she says. 'It wouldn't have mattered who did my job, because it would have happened anyway.

Being there was an extraordinary feeling.'

At the same time as the gifts had been arriving, so did requests for help from evangelical Christians overseas. Tear Fund's first project came to their notice in this way. A Christian mission team in the Chaco region of Argentina appealed for help for the indigenous Indian tribes, and PC1, Project Correspondence 1, was born. The pattern of seeking to help Christians overseas to help their people continued and forms the backbone of Tear Fund's work to this day.

On 29th May 1968, those present at the Relief Fund's first full committee meeting were, as described by Glyn Macaulay,

Mary-Jean Duffield, a fiery LSE graduate; John Boxhall, exactly the opposite, an administrator at London University, who was impeccable – he put us right on many an occasion; myself (his first meeting as chairman); Peter Meadows; Ernest Oliver and Rev George Hoffman. In attendance: Morgan Derham, Mrs Dewdney and Norma Moore.

The fund had already supported projects in Biafra (whose civil war had begun in 1967), the Chaco (Argentina), India, Hong Kong and Jordan. It also helped the well-known missionary Gladys Aylward in Taiwan.

At first it was suggested that the fund keep its present name, 'The EAR Fund', which would provide a convenient slogan, 'Give EAR to the poor'.

Tear Fund was launched with a basic meal contrasting silver candelabra with a typical meal of the poor.

Peter Meadows thought this sounded like a mission to the deaf, so in July 1968 he made a more lasting suggestion, minuted as follows:

Name. It would seem a good time to consider the most suitable name for the fund. Unfortunately the names of Christian organisations tend to shrink to the level of their initials. In choosing the name, this should be borne in mind. The ideal name should be descriptive and also emotive. Proposition: we should adopt the name TEAR Fund.

It was cautiously welcomed, although George Hoffman was concerned that the emotive aspect be held in check. He didn't want tears all over the place; rather, he wanted the Christian public to know what the fund was all about and the biblical reasons for helping those in need.

Peter's first shock-tactic slogan, 'They can't eat prayer', was the theme of the first Tear Fund exhibition stand at the annual Christian holiday crusade at Filey, Yorkshire in September 1968. George and the others thought long and hard before placing these words above the heads of gaunt Vietnamese children with beseeching eyes. The words of Isaiah 1:11–17 made the decision for George: 'What to me are the multitudes of your sacrifices', says the Lord '. . . I have had enough of burnt offerings . . . seek justice, correct oppression, defend the fatherless, plead for the widow . . .'

There was some criticism at the suggestion that prayer was not enough, but the real test came at the second National Assembly of Evangelicals a month later. George gave an address on 'World Poverty and Christian Responsibility':

'This came home to me recently when I heard that in this country there is one doctor to 830 people, whilst in the Indian regions of South America, where Tear Fund has been helping, there is one doctor to 57,000 people. For too long, I believe, we have chosen to ignore hard statistics that speak for themselves: 60 per cent of the population of developing countries suffer from malnutrition. These problems get bigger every year. Last year for instance, there were 70 million more mouths to feed than the year before, but the total amount of food produced was the same.'

Perhaps the statistics are sadly all too familiar now, in our doom-watching society, but they hit home with a freshness then, and the whole address got a tremendous reception. The accompanying resolution was passed unanimously: 'We confess that as Evangelicals we have, to a large extent, failed to realise our social responsibilities and acknowledge our corporate involvement in meeting the physical as well as the spiritual need of men . . .'

(They Can't Eat Prayer by Mary Endersbee, Hodder and Stoughton, London, 1973)

That speech produced letters, telephone calls and gifts for the relief fund; George felt there could be no turning back.

To help convey their special brand of social action to the churches, George Hoffman asked schoolteacher Bill Latham to join Tear Fund as its Education Officer in 1970. At the Evangelical Alliance office in Draycott Place, London, Bill joined a team consisting of 'George, somebody to count the money (Charles Phillimore, the Financial Administrator) and their secretary.' That was Tear Fund, whose total income was around £30,000 that year.

Bill had to educate the Christian public at a time when

the social gospel was considered the terrain of liberals with wishy-washy theology. George understood there was a job of education to be done, of showing the churches that the Bible was not only concerned with man's soul, that God cared about mind, body and soul. It was a matter of redressing the imbalance, of showing that we had a responsibility to feed, to clothe and to educate. Giving dignity and hope were part and parcel of the gospel.

This was the *whole* gospel; not food or salvation alone, but the two together. A saying by Charles Spurgeon has been much quoted: 'If you want to give a hungry man a tract, wrap it in a sandwich.'

The Church received this message with open arms, according to Bill. In fact it was not new, but it revived the spirit of the great evangelical pioneers of the previous century; people like Lord Shaftesbury who campaigned for decent working conditions for children and George Muller who cared for homeless orphans, all committed Christians who championed the poor.

But the fund continued to grow. Bill, although a very able Education Officer, believes it was evident that Tear Fund was God's work from the beginning –

> Otherwise who would have thought it would have grown as it has done? We thought £50,000 was the top whack we'd get in any one year. We'd have laughed if anyone had told us they'd be looking at an income of around £20 million. There were many times in the early days when we'd just stand back and say. 'This is God's doing.' And there are still stories about how God is blessing the work in so many ways.

Bill admits he came into Tear Fund with no knowledge of aid work. 'But I don't know that we needed to know much. It was a straightforward situation of bringing help to people who needed it. We passed money from Christians in Britain to those in the field, so we didn't need to know about the political implications.'

'The whole image of the thing was young,' says Glyn Macaulay.

As chairman, Glyn made trips on Tear Fund's behalf every summer between 1968 and 1975, enjoying the novelty of representing a vigorous young organisation after his long days of accountancy in the City.

'It was so exciting in those days. At an airport in Costa Rica I met a guy who couldn't believe I was who I said I was because he assumed the chairman of a charity would be 95!'

Tear Fund's pioneering work touched a chord in British evangelical Christians: 'People were looking for an opportunity to give,' says Peter Meadows, responsible for Tear Fund's early advertising.

In 1968, it was unusual for evangelicals to become involved in social action. This may be hard to understand, given their response in the late 1980s to the need in Romania and other parts of Eastern Europe, but it is partly due to the example set by Tear Fund that churches see that it is now possible to take aid straight to those in need. While solo efforts are not wholeheartedly endorsed by Tear Fund over and above structured relief programmes, the enthusiasm of the individuals who band together to drive a lorry full of clothes and food to former Yugoslavia owes much to Tear Fund's trail-blazing.

Thanks to the energy shown by Tear Fund and its skilful communication of its work, many have realised that practical caring is not just 'cool'; it says more about their beliefs than sermons ever could.

And the faithful kept growing; for many this was the opportunity to give to those less blessed materially and spiritually, while knowing, from George's reports, exactly where their money was going. Tear Fund projects actually began and ended, so regular contributors could measure the results of their generosity. This accountability appealed to people; it was good to know that your £10 had helped provide water for a village community.

Tear Fund's income almost doubled each year from 1968 onwards, with particular leaps in income matching international crises. By the late 1970s, one man felt Tear Fund had become *too* successful. Morgan Derham, who had served on Tear Fund's board since its birth, says:

> It was capturing the imagination and interest of the younger generation in a way that I felt was tilting the balance too far in the direction of material relief and development programmes. In the 60s, when Tear Fund was gestating, the task was to persuade evangelicals that relief and development work was biblically acceptable – the 'You can't eat prayer' era. But that battle had been largely won, and I felt that the pendulum was swinging too far.

What an irony after the battle to educate the Christian public! But Morgan was right, the Evangelical Alliance Council believed, to suggest the formation of an organisation that would concentrate on spiritual ministries: training in evangelism and leadership for bright potential leaders in overseas churches. After two years' consultation, the new organisation became OECE, the department of Overseas Evangelism and Christian Education, in 1979, assigned to develop within Tear Fund and initially allocated 5 per cent of its grants which was later extended to 10 per cent.

Thus by 1992, £1.3 million had been allocated to OECE to support national Christians in their evangelistic, literature and media initiatives.

The OECE's first director was Ernest Oliver, Associate Director of Tear Fund itself. Ernest had a long and distinguished career as a missionary to Nepal behind him, and was the ideal person to understand the needs of overseas churches keen to provide spiritual direction for their countries. Ernest was succeeded in 1986 by Bill Roberts, another former missionary who had worked for Scripture Union in West Africa.

Recent evangelism and Christian education projects cover most parts of the globe ranging from support for the first Christian university in Romania to supplying a motorbike for a rural evangelist in Africa.

> One of Tear Fund's basic principles states 'the supervision of any Tear Fund supported project is always in the hands of those who want to introduce the people they serve to the "fullness of life" that comes though faith in Jesus Christ alone.'

Tear Fund is now one of Britain's 25 largest charities, with an income of over £20 million a year. Its financial growth is almost entirely the result of voluntary donations from churches and individuals, who had given over £150 million by late 1992. All this happened without Tear Fund itself organising a single public appeal, door-to-door collection or fund-raising event. The core of Tear Fund, says its Communications Director, Stephen Rand, is 'an army of committed individual supporters, whose covenanted giving provides a bedrock of regular support.'

In the months leading up to its 25th anniversary, the leadership of Tear Fund reflected on their future. One result was a straightforward mission statement, stating that the purpose of Tear Fund is 'to serve Jesus Christ by enabling those who share evangelical Christian beliefs to bring good news to the poor'.

This reaffirms Tear Fund's original stance as an evangelical organisation which chooses to focus on its own special constituency – those who believe in a gospel which is good news to the poor.

Stephen Rand explains why Tear Fund is justified in calling its work *Christian* relief and development'. The gospel is for the *whole* person:

While the work of our partners will have many of the features and good practice of relief and development work carried out by dozens of different organisations and charities, it will always have at its heart a concern to communicate the Christian gospel which offers individuals a new relationship with God through Christ, which we believe to be an essential for full and meaningful development.

John Stott, the 'father of British evangelicals' has had a significant impact on the growth of Tear Fund. A close friend of George Hoffman, he had a similar desire to encourage Christians to embrace social action.

He became Tear Fund's first president in 1983 and ten years later accepted the honorary position of Life President. His influence has been considerable, not least expressed through two filmstrips, widely used in churches and student groups.

Word in Action focussed on the biblical principles behind Tear Fund's work, while the earlier *Walk in His Shoes*, made in 1975, was reinforced by a specially written booklet emphasising the example of Jesus for each Christian. Many Tear Fund supporters still point to this filmstrip as a key factor in their decision to get involved with Tear Fund.

> Jesus was not afraid to look human need in the face, in all its ugly reality. And what he saw invariably moved him to compassion, and so to compassionate service. Sometimes, he spoke. But his compassion never dissipated itself in words; it found expression in deeds. He saw, he felt, he acted. The movement was from the eye to the heart, and from the heart to the hand. His compassion was always aroused by the sight of need, and it always led to constructive action.
>
> It seems incontrovertible that if we are even to begin to follow the real Jesus, and to walk in his shoes, we must seize every opportunity to 'do good'. Our good works will show the genuineness of our love, and our love will show the genuineness of our faith.
>
> John R W Stott (*Walk in His Shoes*, 1975)

Partner Portrait

Sami Dagher, Lebanon

Based in Beirut, 56-year-old Sami Dagher is pastor of the Karentina Church.

He and his English wife, Joy, became Christians in the early

1970s under the influence of American missionaries. By his own admission, Sami gave them a hard time.

Patient love and concern won him round and once the about-turn was completed, he and Joy worshipped regularly at the International Church in Muslim West Beirut until the outbreak of civil war in 1975, when they could no longer cross Beirut to reach their church. Instead, they opened their home as a meeting place for three families.

Soon Sami, who had a key position in a prosperous hotel, felt God wanted him to become a full-time minister. In 1976, after fasting and praying, he and Joy started a very small congregation in Karentina, part of the East Beirut docklands, one of the most run-down parts of the city. In 1978 Sami was ordained, and two years later the church was enlarged for the third time to cope with the increasing numbers attending the services. Today there are over 400 people worshipping God in the Karentina Church.

Sami had a vision for church planting, and started another church in Jbeil, near Byblos, 20 miles north of Karentina, which now has 200 members. In early 1993 he opened another church in a Beirut suburb.

Alongside Sami's vision for evangelism has run a conviction that the social cannot be separated from the spiritual ministry. 'If we only give food to the hungry or only preach the gospel, we have failed. Both are commanded by God.'

Their involvement in social action began simply. The area Sami and Joy used to live in was very badly damaged during the war. One afternoon, looking out from their apartment, he saw that the road was pot-holed and full of rubble; in their culture this was unacceptable.

With his son he swept up the mess. Next Sami's family began to distribute clothing to refugee families, and although the Lebanese are a proud people, it was accepted. Many of the families had been made homeless more than once during the fighting.

The next project was rebuilding the lives of two villages. Heavily backed by Tear Fund, the church set about building one decent room in each destroyed home to provide each family with shelter.

Over the years the church has sought to do more than hand out emergency supplies; it also helps people rebuild their lives. Supported by Tear Fund, they built a small sewing and knitting factory above the church youth centre so that 20 of the refugee women could earn their own living. On the Byblos site, the church built 18 homes for refugee families and, backed by an £86,000 grant from Tear Fund, they also built 28 special greenhouses for 14 displaced families, enabling them to support themselves by growing vegetables. The greenhouses, made from simple plastic sheeting and hooped frames, use an advanced Israeli drip system to get the most out of the land while saving on scarce water.

Tear Fund's brand of assistance fitted in perfectly with Sami's vision and his culture, where the people prefer to help themselves rather than receive charity.

'I view both Sami and Joy as vessels used by the Lord,' says Jennie Evans of Tear Fund, who has visited Lebanon regularly since 1977. 'They submit themselves daily to the Lord's will and place themselves under his protection.'

God's protection has been much valued, both by Sami's family and the church. 'Every believer in the church could tell you a story of God's goodness and protection,' says Sami. His own daughter, Anna, one night had a bullet pass right through her pyjama trousers, yet she remained unharmed. Sami has twice narrowly escaped being kidnapped. On one occasion he recalled,

I was put in one room alone, and I was very afraid. I took out my pocket New Testament, but my hands were shaking so much that I couldn't even see the words. I knelt down and said, 'Lord help mo', from the bottom of my heart. I stopped shaking and experienced the peace of God which passes all understanding.

Amazingly, he was released unharmed. Much negotiation had gone on between his church and the kidnappers. A week later Sami returned to them with a Bible and a letter of thanks for his release.

The TEAR FUND Story

Year	Description	Annual Income
1968 BIAFRA Civil war in Nigeria leads to terrible famine – hunger on TV news	The decision is taken to develop EAR Fund and present it to the public under the leadership of the Rev George Hoffman. 'The' is added, and Refugee becomes Relief – hence The Evangelical Alliance Relief Fund – TEAR Fund. The first ever grant is made to a development programme in Argentina.	£34,000
1969	Cliff Richard gives his first Tear Fund concert in the Royal Albert Hall.	£55,000
1970 CYCLONE Tidal wave in East Pakistan	Tear Fund links up with a Christian organisation in India and a missionary society to send help to East Pakistan. Money is given to support two missionaries working in development in Africa.	£88,000
1971 CIVIL WAR Pakistan divides and Bangladesh is born	A record is produced to tell churches and youth groups about the refugee situation in Calcutta, and help is given for 20,000 people.	£208,000
1972	Tear Fund helps to start HEED Bangladesh and ACROSS in Sudan – groups of Christian organisations working together to bring relief and development in the wake of civil war.	£271,000
1973 DROUGHT In India twenty million people face starvation: in Ethiopia drought threatens government	The support of skilled people sent to help in emergencies is developed into a new department at Tear Fund now called Overseas Personnel, selecting and sending doctors, builders, agriculturalists, etc., to various countries. Water drilling rigs are sent to India and Ethiopia.	£542,000
1974	Tear Fund supporters are given the opportunity to give £5 per month to sponsor children in Christian orphanages in Bangladesh, providing food, health care and education. This later grows into the Partners in Childcare Scheme.	£907,000
1975	The determination to help people to help themselves leads to Tearcraft, which begins by bringing jute goods from Bangladesh for sale in Britain. This develops into a handicraft import business owned by Tear Fund, which helps to provide employment for thousands of skilled workers.	£1,221,000

1976 EARTHQUAKE 22,000 dead in Guatemala	Largest-yet response to a special appeal following Guatemala earthquake. Increasing support at home encourages Tear Fund to open regional offices in Belfast and Glasgow.	**£1,247,000**
1977 CYCLONE Disaster in India claims 85,000 people	The on-going relationship with the Evangelical Fellowship of India means that Tear Fund is able to respond to its largest ever request for development help after the cyclone disaster: £100,000.	**£1,695,000**
1978	The Youth and Student Section starts to help young people know more about Tear Fund. The Tearaways club for young children is launched. Cliff Richard includes a special concert in his fund-raising tour to celebrate Tear Fund's tenth birthday.	**£2,162,000**
1979 REFUGEE CRISIS in South East Asia Vietnamese Boat People pour into Hong Kong. Cambodians flee terror and enter Thailand	Tear Fund takes on extensive work in the refugee camps of Hong Kong and Thailand. Discussions with various evangelical groups in Britain lead to a new department —Overseas Evangelism and Christian Education – which supports the rapidly growing churches of the developing world.	**£3,289,000**
1980 SOMALIA 1½ million refugees from Ethiopian War	Somalia has no Christian churches, so Tear Fund takes the unusual step of sending its own medical team to work in two of the refugee camps.	**£3,949,000**
1981	Tear Fund sends its first full-time administrators overseas to work in East Africa, which has become an important focus for projects and personnel.	**£4,541,000**
1982 LEBANON The continuing conflict: fighting intensifies	Cliff Richard helps Tear Fund to make its first film, *Cliff in Kenya*. Tearcraft launches Tear Fund Tea, grown on a Christian-run tea plantation in North East India. A major relief programme in Beirut and southern Lebanon meets with a generous response from Christians in Britain.	**£5,597,000**
1983	A special presentation called *Road To Freedom* and featuring Garth Hewitt visits 24 towns in Britain to emphasise how Christians should respond to the needs of others.	**£6,402,000**

1984
ETHIOPIA
Ten million face
starvation – the
television nightmare
from Africa

A new scheme to encourage long-term
support of development programmes is
launched, called 'Partners in
Development'. Tear Fund supporters
respond rapidly and generously
to the Ethiopian crisis. A 24-hour telephone
service offers information for those who
pray for the work of Tear Fund.　　**£11,178,000**

1985
LIVE AID
The biggest
ever charity event
spans the world

The *Candle in the Darkness* presentation is
seen by 33,000 people in 42 towns in Britain. It
is designed to help Christians think about
how best to celebrate Christmas in
a world of desperate need.　　**£10,289,000**

1986

A new scheme to help church representatives
is launched, aiming to keep churches
informed and involved in caring for
the poor.　　**£10,784,000**

1987

Tear Fund is asked to take responsibility for
the education and healthcare of thousands
of Cambodian refugee children in Thailand. **£12,250,000**

1988
SUDAN
Floods make 1
million homeless

£104,000 is allocated to the Sudan Interior
Church to distribute emergency supplies,
following floods. Tear Fund nurse Heather
Sinclair is abducted by Sudanese rebels and
kept captive for 49 days. Devastating
earthquake hits Armenia. £59,000 is given
immediately to care for the victims.　　**£14,187,000**

1989
REVOLUTION
Turmoil in Eastern
Europe

The Berlin Wall comes down, and revolution in Romania leads to downfall of Ceausescu. Tear Fund contributes a total of £46,700 towards relief efforts. Weekend for the World and youth resource *3rd Track* are launched in Tear Fund's 21st year   .£14,439,000

1990
EARTHQUAKES

Earthquakes devastate areas of the Philippines, Iran and Peru. In Iran up to 50,000 people die. Tear Fund's partners in all three countries are able to respond. Many Christians in Nepal are freed after political reforms are introduced. Tear Fund, working with Youth for Christ introduces *Through Different Eyes*, taking young UK Christians to Third World locations to learn with national Christians the meaning of the Gospel.   £15,423,000

1991
GULF WAR

Tear Fund provides shelter for 100,000 Kurdish and Iraqi refugees in the wake of the Gulf War. A Tear Fund team goes to work in Northern Iraq and appears on *Songs of Praise*. Grants totalling £117,000 are made to the emergency relief fund after Mount Pinatubo erupts in the Philippines. Tear Fund introduces the Bread for Life programme to support feeding programmes as well as tackling the root causes of famine.   £19,510,000

1992
DROUGHT
Thousands of lives
threatened in
Africa

The WHOSE EARTH? initiative is begun, linked with Spring Harvest – an environmental project for young Christians, in association with Spring Harvest. 3,000 attend the 'Picnic for the World' in Hyde Park. As severe drought hits Africa, Tear Fund gives over £2 million towards famine relief. Yugoslavia is torn apart by civil war. £55,000 is given to help the victims of 'ethnic cleansing'.   £22,000,000

CHAPTER THREE

GEORGE HOFFMAN
1933–1992

Perhaps the most telling indication of the importance of George Hoffman's role with Tear Fund is the fact that few of those who flocked to pay tribute after his untimely death on 16th October 1992 bothered to name his role with Tear Fund. They were convinced that for thousands of supportive Christians up and down Britain and overseas, George *was* Tear Fund.

From the day he was handed a file named 'Relief Funds' by his then boss, Evangelical Alliance General Secretary Morgan Derham, George had found his calling. He would not have seen it as a calling. For him, it was simple, biblical obedience to care for his fellow man. John's verses emphasising the importance of reflecting your love for God in your treatment of your neighbour summed up George's view of God and the world: 'And he has given us this command: Whoever loves God must also love his brother.' (1 John 4:21)

Morgan Derham was to explain at the service of thanksgiving for George's life over 20 years later,

> George's whole life was committed to putting that 'also' into our Christianity. Evangelical Christians have always made a great deal of the personal relationship with God – and rightly – but when, back in '67, we began to plan what became eventually Tear Fund, we had a very simple mission. It was to inject that 'brother also' into the thinking and living of the evangelical churches. It may surprise you, but you couldn't take it for granted then.
>
> And then George came and in a very extraordinary way proved to be the man for the task, because for him, 'also' was the very heart of his view of God and the world. As a result of the work he did, I think it's fair to say that loving our brother 'also' has been burnt into the consciences of the churches and their members.

The Evangelical Alliance broadsheet of 1967 carried a photo of a youthful Morgan Derham on its cover, with the following announcement inside:

> The Rev George Hoffman, formerly Senior Curate of Edgware Parish Church, has joined the staff as Assistant Secretary of

the Evangelical Alliance. Mr Hoffman is taking further editorial responsibilities at headquarters, including press relationships and publicity, besides continuing as Assistant Editor of *Crusade* magazine. He has also taken on editing the new-look broadsheet. In addition, he will be responsible for a number of specialised projects, such as the Relief Fund, which is being widely publicised this winter.

In May 1968, Glyn Macaulay arrived at his first committee meeting of the Relief Fund, in response to a request from Morgan Derham to act as the fund's accountant. 'I had the first of the Hoffman handshakes and greetings,' he recalls. 'As the hand came out and the eyes pierced straight into mine and the hand grasped my arm in the way that George always did, I suddenly realised that it was the same Hoffman who was a very pale-looking guy a couple of years ahead of me at Birkenhead School.'

George's pallor belied his vigour. Glyn was to receive several letters over the years, firmly asking him to look after his Executive Director in the same way that Tear Fund looked after the poor and starving around the world, 'because he looks ill'.

In fact George worked hard at whatever he undertook, but the nervous energy expended required adequate amounts of rest. Those invited to parties at George and Pauline's Ealing house in the early 1970s recall playing carefully prepared party games, identifying the products behind torn-out newspaper advertisements and television jingles. There was plenty of food and fun, Glyn Macaulay remembers.

> But just when we thought the party was halfway through, George would get his *Daily Light* out, read a few words and pray. Then he pushed off to bed, wanting to be up at his usual unearthly hour to read the Word. We'd carry on with the party until we heard bangs on the ceiling as George tried desperately to get some sleep.

Bill Latham, who travelled a great deal with George, also learned a lot from him about conserving energy for the important business in hand. In the plane for a long-haul journey to Asia, or in the back of a host's car, George caught up on his sleep. Once awake again, in time for the real work of the day, George was an amusing companion, his Merseyside wit a surprising asset in defusing the mounting emotions of those unused to witnessing scenes of suffering. Travelling companions like Bill Latham, Tony Neeves and Garth Hewitt remember roaring with laughter over ridiculous incidents, a laughter that was necessary for equilibrium in the circumstances they saw people facing, rather than disregard for those circumstances. After long, tiring days meeting people and assessing needs, George gave of himself again, inspiring the Tear Fund nurses and engineers, or whichever Christian workers were present, through Bible studies and encouraging them to keep going.

And of course there were tears as well as laughter. At Glyn Macaulay's insistence, George had agreed to visit Calcutta in August 1971. His subsequent report, released on a floppy vinyl record to supporters, became the first of many which alerted the Christian public to suffering in the Third World. Ironically, in view of George's desire to educate rather than elicit an emotional response in his listeners, the report's evidently restrained emotion drew an unrestrained response from its listeners; the report was a very British response to tragedy.

> We've been visiting a hospital in a refugee camp outside Calcutta. As a result, one of those horrible silences has settled over us as we drive out of the camp now. As we stood by one ward a man collapsed in front of us as he was being brought in by his relatives. He was in the advanced stages of cholera. Five people died yesterday in that ward alone, of cholera. In the same place five babies were born.
>
> The mothers held up before us their little babies that looked as though they were dying. The tears were streaming down their faces as they reached over the barbed wire to where we stood . . .
>
> I wondered all of a sudden why I couldn't move my legs. I found there was a woman wrapped around them, holding my feet and kissing them, refusing to let them go. Tears ran down her face . . . It is very hard on such an occasion not to weep also, and throw down every penny you've got.
>
> It's strange. When we left Calcutta this morning, the conversation in this truck was animated. Ever since we left the camp there has been hardly a word spoken. We are just sitting, strong, grown men, with watery eyes, finding it very difficult to talk . . .

It is hard to over-estimate George Hoffman's contribution to Tear Fund's growth. His abilities as a journalist, allied to his vision for helping those who could not help themselves, was largely responsible for Tear Fund's attracting support from the Christian public. *Tear Times* under George's editorship was ablaze with all the conviction of a revolutionary broadsheet; it was unashamedly partisan, a rallying call to the faithful to *do something* about the causes set before them.

His 'unparalleled gift of communication', to quote his old friend Bill Spencer, now editor of *Evangelism Today*, was employed not only in print but in meetings at churches throughout Britain.

George wedded a heart of compassion to words that drove people to respond. In troubled spots around the world he visited, assessed the needs, and made the vital contacts with key Christians. He quickly came to the conclusion that whatever the need, God had someone who could become involved. He marvelled at the way he found dedicated followers of Christ in every part of the globe. It was enough to make a proud man humble; in George it just created an extra well of love for the God who made it happen, and for his servants, who frequently reduced him to tears by the beauty of their lives. It was this George Hoffman that came back again and again and in telling phrases and with soulful eyes gave his witness.

(Evangelism Today, November 1992)

'George loved people as individuals,' says Peter Meadows. 'He didn't love the world en masse, dispassionately; his love overflowed to all those individuals. He wasn't simply a pioneer who loved doing big projects, but a pioneer who acted boldly.'

Those who volunteered for overseas service met a man who was their pastor and friend, who took them toothpaste and chocolate (a contradictory but highly-valued combination for young Britons abroad). Among the many who felt his loss is Liz Wilkinson, who worked as a nurse in Bangladesh.

> George has been a spiritual father, a mentor, to me. He supported me when our second child died – he was a tremendous help – and he's just been somebody who was always there in the background. There was a great sense of loss when he died. He had a tremendous vision with the gift of communication to express it. Just two weeks before he was killed he came to speak to our home group about the situation in Croatia. There were about 40 people in my friends' home and they were just mesmerised with the way he could portray a situation.

George was able to bring back vivid images which captured the most under-used imagination. His listeners' usual response, as in Liz's home group, was 'How can we help?' Liz and her friends had an advance Christmas collection, gathering not only money but toiletries, bedding and clothes for a convoy to Croatia.

George never forgot that God was responsible for Tear Fund's growth, but as Tear Fund grew, its *modus operandi* necessarily changed. At the beginning it had been perfectly appropriate for George to hop on a plane in response to a cry for help, assess the situation, speak his impressions into his dictaphone for *Tear Times* and send a cheque on his return. After all, it was his responsiveness, his dedication to the causes above even his family, that had pushed Tear Fund into the big league as a charity. His wife Pauline and their daughters not only contributed by releasing George in this way; Pauline herself worked at Tear Fund, for many years as Personnel Manager, striving to maintain a strong sense of family feeling for all who worked at Tear Fund, even as the numbers grew and grew.

But with so many new projects starting up all the time, the

On October 31st 1989, George Hoffman was awarded the Order of the British Empire for his services to the cause of the underprivileged in the Third World. He is seen here with his wife Pauline, shortly after having received his OBE.

organisation had to grow, adapt and change. There had to be procedures and joint decisions. George was more of a leader than a manager, yet he put in place the appropriate management structure enabling him to delegate.

Indeed, Tear Fund's success as a charity was ready proof that he and others had been put by God into the right place at the right time. In his *Tear Times* editorial of spring 1986, three and a half years before his service to Tear Fund ended, he wrote:

> Over the years we have had a maxim in Tear fund: 'God's method is God's man' (in the generic sense – bearing in mind that most of our overseas workers have been women!) This, we believe has good Bible precedents. And the Christian church has followed a similar pattern over the years. When God wants to do something he raises up a person. He doesn't, as somebody has put it, appoint a committee. Come to think of it, I have yet to see a monument to a committee. And God's person is normally characterised by a God-given vigour, and a God-given vision.

In that piece George went on to attribute these qualities to his old college principal, Rev J Stafford Wright, but nine years later they have the poignancy of an advance obituary written by George about himself.

Tear Fund consultant David Primrose presented a profile of the man who never failed to put compassion before committees.

> George was a visionary, a feather on the breath of God, one for whom Christ-centred compassion drove him to serve far beyond his own capacities. Such total commitment brought its associated problems, as the people of God struggled to support such a highly individualistic ministry. Those who had personally benefited from his ministry responded with a loyalty born out of gratitude. Associates and colleagues who had to cope with what appeared to them as errors of judgement struggled hard to integrate their hard-bitten wisdom with George's spiritual inspiration.
>
> George's sensitivity to the movement of the Spirit, and his genuine love for individuals, inspired a deep loyalty amongst those who received his ministry. He did not encourage others to remain dependent on him, but pointed them to their Saviour. George found it more difficult to involve others in his inner process of decision-making, often presenting friends and supporters with dramatic *fait-accomplis.'*

George became General Director but in 1988 the Board terminated his twenty years of fruitful service. A year later he became the Executive Chairman in Europe of Samaritan International, in partnership with Billy Graham's son Franklin. Once again George was able to fly into a trouble spot, assess the needs and make a practical, personal response.

Before his death George had been deeply involved in Bosnia, working with his long-time friend and Tear Fund partner Branko Lovrec. When Branko heard of George's untimely death, he mourned: 'I have lost my brother; I have lost my soul-mate; I have lost my friend.'

On the night of his death, George was travelling to Gloucester to speak at a weekend arranged by four local Baptist churches. He was to stay with Nick Carr, now retired from his ministry with the Overseas Missionary Fellowship. George was on the wrong road and telephoned Nick for new directions. Nick takes up the story:

> He followed them and came under a bridge as he should, but overshot a bit and stopped his car and went over the road to check exactly where he was. There were three houses opposite, and he chose to go to the middle one. I've since spoken to the lady who advised him, and found she is a charming Christian lady who knew of George and his work. In fact her home is full of goods ready to go out to Eastern Europe. She was the last person to speak to him.
>
> As he crossed the road, no doubt bothered that he was so late getting to us and the meeting, he didn't notice the Renault coming the other way. George was taken to the hospital but never recovered. What can we say? God is sovereign, and

we must say that God had decided that George's work here was ended.

Many, like Liz Wilkinson, believe that George Hoffman was God's voice to challenge Christians about the world's poor while bringing God's encouragement to Christians trying to redeem appalling situations overseas. His drive and sincerity lit the flame of hope in their hearts while mobilising an army of givers at home. 'Whatever organisation George had been working for, regardless of the name, he would be speaking God's message. It didn't really matter who he was working for; he was working for God.'

Call us, Lord, to take up the torch which George Hoffman laid down and to hold it even higher and firmer because of his example and challenge.

(From John Stott's prayer at George Hoffman's thanksgiving service, 30th January, 1993)

Cliff admired George tremendously according to Bill Latham, and I think a lot of what George was and all that he stood for actually rubbed off on other people, which is why there was such shock at his death. A lot of us actually caught some of his in-depth commitment and passion, so one feels a little bit of George is in me, and a little bit of George is in Cliff.

EMPLOYMENT

'Progress' in the western world sometimes spells disaster as machines take over the work that used to be done by people in the poorer countries. The discovery of a new synthetic material is not quite the technological breakthrough it appears to be, if its use means no work for a people whose product is no longer required.

Tear Fund sees the provision of work as a priority in the poorer countries and every encouragement is given to labour intensive employment schemes using appropriate technology.

Unemployment Rate

6 per cent of the UK labour force can find no work. But in the developing world, many countries have an unemployment rate higher than 25 per cent. And in those places where 1 in 4 or even 1 in 3 are out of work there is no social security–just grinding poverty and very little hope.

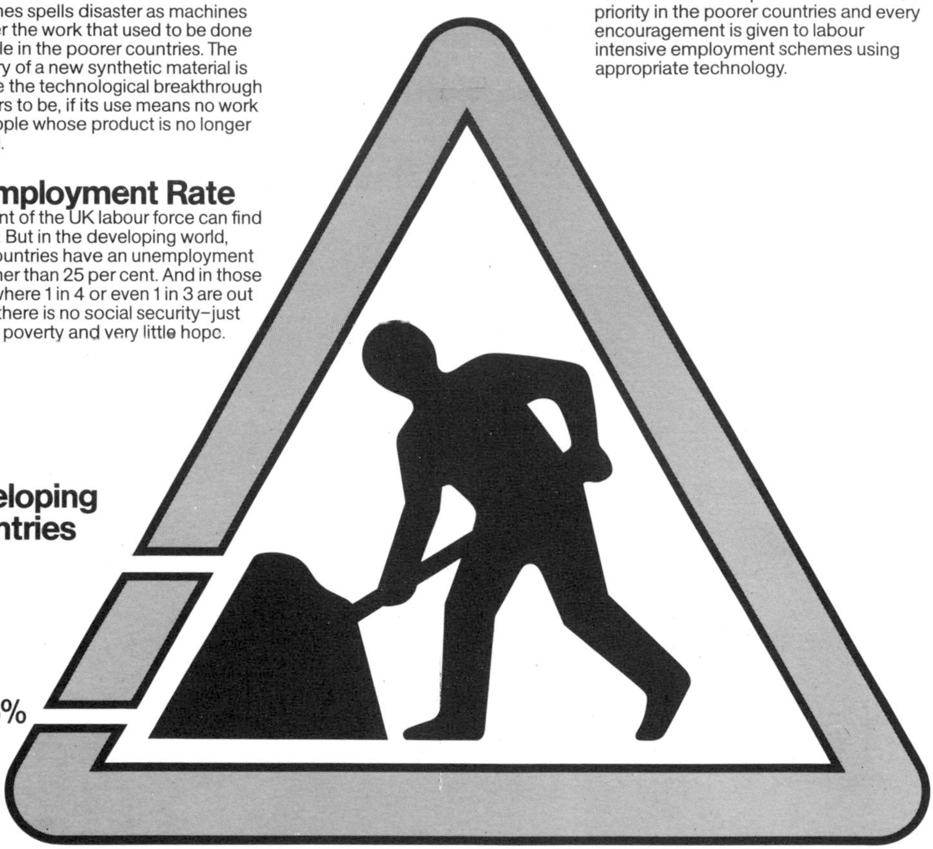

Developing Countries 25%
UK 6%

Percentage of Population Without Adequate Employment, Unemployed or Underemployed*

(*Underemployed – those with only casual or part-time work, usually yielding inadequate income.)

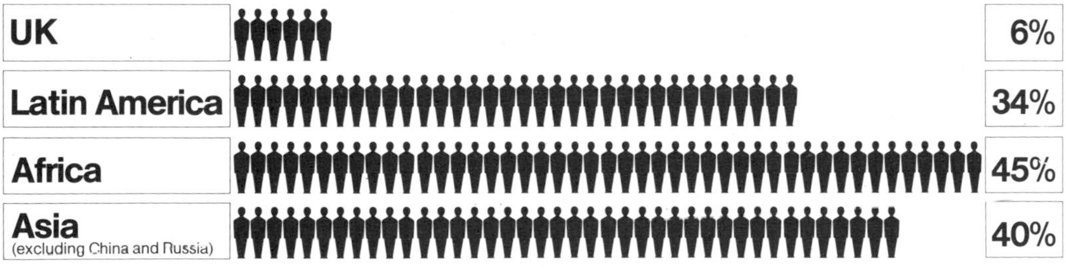

UK
6%
Latin America
34%
Africa
45%
Asia
(excluding China and Russia)
40%

"There is nothing better for a man than that he should eat and drink and find enjoyment in his work." ***Eccl 2:24***

TEAR FUND

HEALTH

One-third of the world's population have no facilities for the disposal of sewage and waste: this is a major health hazard. Ignorance of the basic hygiene and feeding needs of babies causes millions of unnecessary deaths each year.

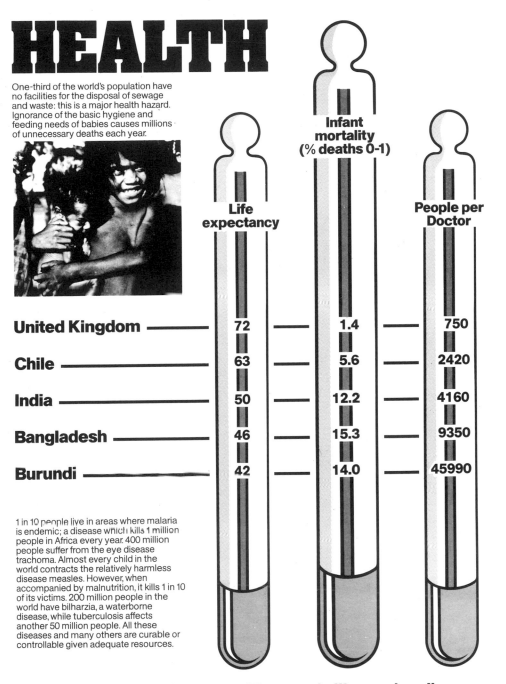

	Life expectancy	Infant mortality (% deaths 0-1)	People per Doctor
United Kingdom	72	1.4	750
Chile	63	5.6	2420
India	50	12.2	4160
Bangladesh	46	15.3	9350
Burundi	42	14.0	45990

1 in 10 people live in areas where malaria is endemic; a disease which kills 1 million people in Africa every year. 400 million people suffer from the eye disease trachoma. Almost every child in the world contracts the relatively harmless disease measles. However, when accompanied by malnutrition, it kills 1 in 10 of its victims. 200 million people in the world have bilharzia, a waterborne disease, while tuberculosis affects another 50 million people. All these diseases and many others are curable or controllable given adequate resources.

"Jesus went about all the cities and villages healing every disease and every infirmity."
Mt 9:35

CHAPTER FOUR

GOOD NEWS TO THE POOR

'A Third World situation in a First World country' was how *Tear Times* described the living conditions of the 50,000 aboriginal Indians of the Argentine Chaco in 1977.

The Chaco, a desolate bush area in the north of Argentina, spreading into Bolivia and Paraguay, is home to two Indian tribes living along the banks of the River Pilcomayo, prone to flooding the Indians' villages.

Over the last 25 years, Tear Fund has allocated a total of £900,000 to the work in the Chaco. The money has gone on land purchase, training, equipment, water improvement and bee-keeping, as well as detailed social welfare, health and education programmes.

Traditionally these Indian tribes lived by seasonal fishing, hunting and gathering in the bush. But fish were no longer plentiful, the forests were devoid of animals, and the Indians were living in a state of semi-starvation, with an appallingly high incidence of diseases like TB and measles. Jim Muggleton, a Tear Fund water engineer, saw several babies and children dying in a whooping cough epidemic. In fact, Tear Fund had been involved in the region since 1968, and

by 1977 several Tear Fund-supported workers were living amongst the Indians. Peter Tyson and his wife, nurse Margaret Grebby and dentist Rob Munday and his wife were based at La Paz, a river settlement described by Jim as one of the most unattractive and inhospitable places he had ever seen. They were living in mud-brick houses in a squalid Indian village, where dust storms were frequent. The ground, Jim said, was 'covered in a dark brown talcum powder, which had the consistency of wet cocoa when it rained'.

Temperatures rose to 120 degrees in the summer and there were no roads through the Chaco, only tracks. No one undertook a journey without carrying two days' water supply, a winch, four spare wheels, patches and a tool box. Jim recalled that:

> The plight of the Indian tribes is pathetic. They are being edged out, on the one hand by go-getting Argentinian white farmers with modern technology who are clearing the forests on the south side of the Chaco, and on the other hand, by the non-viability of their traditional way of life.
>
> The answers to their problems are not easy, but, amidst the appalling conditions, Tear Fund workers, with their host missionary society SAMS (South American Missionary Society), are showing an understanding of the Indians' plight, are helping them make the transition without which they would probably face extinction, and, above all, are caring because God cares.

Peter Tyson believed that the answer was to persuade the Indians to abandon their old way of life and to take up farming, but this has been an uphill struggle. They had lived from day to day by hunting and fishing for centuries, and the long-term cycle of farming had little appeal.

That same year, 1977, Tear Fund agriculturalist Chris Hawksbee went with his wife Alison to help the Indians. Sixteen years later, after many assignments and different experiences he is still there.

The son of missionary parents, born in Paraguay, Chris regards himself as a South American and closely identifies with the Chaco Indians. This is a blessing, as is Chris's patience. 'He patiently teaches the Indians all he knows and waits to see it put into practice because he has a very strong sense that the Chaco is where God wants him to be,' explains a Tear Fund manager. Chris puts it more simply: 'I love them very much and they love me.'

Changing times in the Chaco

All projects supported by Tear Fund were given a PC number – PC stood for Project Correspondence. PC1 was the Argentinian Chaco. In 1968 money went tc help the Anglican Church's medical programme at a time when nearly half of all Indian children were dying before their fifth birthday.

When missionaries from SAMS made their first contact with the Indians in 1911, the beliefs of the Indians were animistic, which meant they lived in fear of evil spirits. They also knew what it meant to be exploited, both by working on the estates of colonialists and by being forced from their traditional hunting grounds onto marginal lands.

The work made a significant leap forward in 1914 in the Paraguayan area of the Chaco. Henry Grubb arrived – a missionary whose steel-rimmed spectacles inspired the Indians to call him *Techinas*, 'Iron Eyes'. Having established a relationship of trust and care with the Paraguayan Indians, the Church invited Grubb to Northern Argentina to make contact with the Matacho tribe.

The work grew steadily, establishing schools and clinics, as well as bringing the gospel to the Indians. But the Indians' marginal position in their land deteriorated, until in 1970 they turned to the Anglican Church in desperation and pleaded with them to obtain land they could call their own. Their church leaders were also concerned about the cultural and moral disintegration of their communities, due to the migration of young people to the white towns and plantations, where they were absorbed into the lowest social stratum. Since the church leaders were also tribal leaders, they needed to see their communities preserved if they were to serve them. They wanted jobs to be created within their traditional homeland which would be more attractive to their young people than employment elsewhere.

The Church agreed, and created four settlements covering a total area of around 170 square miles, on which the majority of the Indians lived.

At first, the Church had ambitious plans for the region. In 1972 they set up Iniciativa Cristiana (Christian Initiative) with a ten-year plan to combat poverty in the area, creating work opportunities through agriculture, crafts and industry. They hoped to hand over entirely to the Indians at the end of this time.

The Chaco was the region which benefited from Cliff Richard's very first concerts in aid of Tear Fund on 15th and 16th January, 1969. It was a considerable act of faith for a fledgling charity less than a year old to take on London's largest concert hall, the Royal Albert Hall, for two nights, even with such a star attraction as Cliff, but faith was rewarded with an attendance of 7,500 people over the two nights, raising £800 towards the cost of a Land Rover for use in the Chaco.

After two farms failed (the river flooded and they were too remote), the Indians were encouraged to move their families to border-zone areas and to work on the farms there, with improved housing, schools and medical services.

By 1980, however, Iniciativa Cristiana realised that the communities had become too dependent on the help of the foreigners. There was a 1,000 worker farm, but the Indians were not solely responsible for it. They were having to work in totally new ways, with the farm perhaps concentrating too much on cash crops and large-scale machinery.

In response, a committee of Indian leaders was set up to take part in decision making. They also moved away from large-scale programmes, which needed constant funding, towards smaller projects which would be easier for the Indians to sustain without outside help.

The Falklands war in 1982 coincided with the end of the ten-year plan; now the ex-patriates had to leave, whether or not it was convenient for the project's management. In fact it became a turning point, as the Indians were forced to take a greater responsibility for the work.

The whole experience has been a milestone in understanding the best way to help a developing race; it has even inspired three people to write theses about the work in the Chaco!

Kevin McKemey, Project Director for Iniciativa Cristiana for ten years, is one of those people. When he first went to the Chaco, he discovered the Indians had little respect for their own indigenous status within Argentine society. 'They were marginalised socially, psychologically, politically, culturally and ethnically. The white society was also discriminatory towards them. So their approach to agriculture was to seek a *patron*, someone they could work under.'

Growing confidence in their own identity meant that the Indians began to challenge their committee of leaders, demanding their own tribal representatives. Soon it was realised they were much better motivated working within their own clans (tribal sub-divisions), and new projects were devised accordingly.

One of the new, smaller and sustainable projects was bee-keeping, in which Chris Hawksbee started to train families before the Falklands war. During the crisis the Hawksbees moved to Paraguay, where the success of their bee-keeping encouraged them to re-establish the project on their return to Argentina in 1989. Chris started to train two local young men to continue the project, along-side other agricultural projects. In the Tear Fund video *Good News to the Poor*, Chris is seen working with the Indians he loves. One bee-keeping project has brought in such healthy profits that the men asked Chris for all the equipment he had, but Chris had to deny them. 'It would be easy to spoil them, but no good for their dignity.'

A farming project – clan-based, of course – has also been success-ful. The Indians grow traditional crops: pumpkins, sweet potatoes, melons and water-melons. 'To make money in farming you have to be ahead of everyone else,' explains Chris. 'The best thing I can teach them is how to commercialise things and not accept just any price for their crops.'

Some anthropologists have been critical of missionaries, but the impact of missionaries in the Chaco has been positive and fruitful, preserving the Indian communities, even though Kevin and the others encountered some misunderstanding from the authorities during the 1970s – happily 'indigenous differentiation' is not considered subver-sive by the current government. The success of the programme was proved by the fact that many more young people were staying in their homeland by the time Kevin's service ended; they even had reverse migration – young people returning to their homeland.

'The big impact made by the missions was to change both the indigenous communities' evaluation of themselves and the white society's view of the Indians, once they were seen to be capable of using their land profitably.'

Chris Hawksbee has also made a key discovery in his years with the Indians: 'The most enthusiastic Christians are the most successful farmers!' He feels that they care for each other, for the land, and are motivated to make the most of their meagre resources. The majority of the Indians have come to know Christ, and been freed of their fear of evil spirits. As Bishop Maurice Sinclair, director of the Anglican programme, said,

> The impact of the gospel is not always obvious but it is profound. Previously the Indians were a nomadic people. With the arrival of the Spanish-speaking settlers, they were scattered and disorientated. The gospel has stabilised their community life, and enabled them to regroup and reform their lives.

He believes the gospel must be preached, lived and taught, and in the late 1980s introduced a new emphasis to the Anglican Church's social programme among the Indians; they would 'go deeper in Christian education, applying the gospel to every area of the people's lives – community life, money, work, health – all these things which are very central to the concerns of Tear Fund.'

For instance in 1971 two young couples went out to serve the Indians of the Argentine Chaco as agricultural missionaries. Peter and Frances Tyson and Kevin and Denise McKemey were sent out by SAMS (South American Missionary Society) while Tear Fund undertook their financial support.

Kevin McKemey was to stay with the project, becoming director of Iniciativa Cristiana, one of the largest rural development programmes that Tear Fund has ever supported. In 1985, Kevin became Tear Fund's Consultant on Vocational Training and Small Industries. 'He has a way of looking at development which gets straight to the heart of the matter,' reported his colleague John Townsend, then Director of Overseas Support Services.

Later Kevin took a Master's degree in Community Development and was invited to join World Relief in the USA as its Latin American Regional Director. In 1991 he became a part-time consultant to World Relief in order to finish his PhD on the social consequences of rainforest management systems. Born and brought up in East Africa, he plans to continue working overseas after gaining his doctorate.

Human Rights

In many parts of the world, the Church is learning to stand with people whose rights to land and security are violated. Whether it is the victims of state and terrorist violence in Peru, or the indigenous Indians of Central and South America, Tear Fund supports the Church as it seeks freedom for the oppressed.

Partner Portrait

Bishop Mario Marino

'Projects come. Projects go. But *we* remain. The people!' Bishop Mario told *Tear Times* in 1982. The first Indian bishop of the Anglican Church in the Chaco, he lives among his people in a group of adobe buildings in the centre of an Indian encampment.

Life has changed enormously for the latest generation of young people, whom the missionaries worked so hard to retain, and Bishop Mario is in a unique position to help them because he combines cultural sensitivity with the love of Christ.

'We need to apply the teaching of the Bible to today's needs, because there are so many outside influences,' he told journalist Paul Clark during the making of the Tear Fund video *Good News to the Poor* in 1991. 'The old people lived in the bush. They hunted and gathered. Young people now have TVs and videos, so we have to be more professional in the preparation of Bible teaching materials.'

He is convinced that the local people should run their own church in that part of Argentina. 'It is very important for them to be at ease, expressing release and feelings in their way without any sort of binding from outside.'

In 1992, the 500th anniversary of Columbus' discovery of America was celebrated. With no delusions about the atrocities committed against the Indians by the white man from 1492 onwards, Bishop Mario worked with other Indian leaders to draw up a document forgiving the white man all the wrong he had done, and expressing their commitment to working together for the future. This wise act symbolises the determination of Bishop Mario to leave past wrongs and past mistakes behind as he works towards a better, dignified future for his people:

'We need prayer that the Church will be strong so that they can guide the people forward, especially with all the political changes and the corruption in politics. Pray that the Church will be the light to lead the whole of the Indian community forward, whether they are Christian or non-Christian.'

CHAPTER 5

THEY CAN'T EAT PRAYER

Living at starvation level for nearly two years was not what Bill Roberts had in mind when he achieved a long-time desire to work in Nigeria.

MIG fighters – bombs – rockets – starving refugees – dead bodies . . . That was never my idea of missionary work. Preaching and teaching – even a certain amount of hardship if necessary – but not fighting to keep starving children just alive, escaping death literally by minutes, coping with military interrogation – and watching how God handled impossible circumstances, so that in spite of the death all around them, hundreds of young men and women could find the new kind of life that He gives.
(*Life and Death Among the Ibos*, Scripture Union, London, 1970)

Bill spent a year at London Bible College before applying to be a Scripture Union travelling secretary in Nigeria, teaching and training Scripture Union groups in schools and universities. Similar in operation to Christian Unions in Britain, new SU groups had to be initiated, and existing ones nurtured.

From 1964 to 1967 his lifestyle was what he had expected in eastern Nigeria, a region which considered itself mainly Christian. In his visits to schools Bill found that the main problem was nominal Christianity; he longed to see young people fully living the Christian life.

He had been there two years when the country was plunged into a bitter civil war. Bill was regional secretary for the south-east, the area inhabited by the Ibos, a minority tribe noted for their entrepreneurial abilities and high level of education.

Rumbling unrest exploded into hostilities when the Ibos, mistrustful of the rest of the country, especially the Hausa-dominated north, seceded from the Nigerian Federation, declaring the formation of the independent republic of Biafra on 30th May 1967.

Very soon fighting started between the Ibos and the Nigerian army, composed mainly of the other two dominant tribes, the Hausas from the north and Yorubas from the south-west. Biafra, an area of 15 million people, squared up to the rest of Nigeria's 100 million inhabitants on its own.

Bill was left with some hard decisions. Should he stay or leave? If he stayed, what was he to do? 'We were instructed by our governments to leave, but some of us felt we had a higher authority in such a critical situation.' Bill was 32 when war broke out, relatively fit and without family responsibilities.

Holding onto the risen Jesus' promise at the end of Matthew's gospel, 'Lo, I am with you always', Bill made his lonely decision to stay.

Everywhere there was fear, as the Nigerian army blockaded the coast and formed a tight ring round Biafra's borders. The schools and colleges soon closed down, leaving thousands of young people with time on their hands. At this early stage, Bill received one touching confirmation that he was needed among his adopted people.

> Lots of students came down to the house to see if I was still there. When they saw I was, their faces just lit up with tremendous joy that I hadn't left them in their hour of need. After that, all the keen young Christians kept on coming to my house and we naturally prayed together, studied the Bible together and sang together.

There could be no formal SU work during the war. But as word got around that Bill had stayed, so more young people started coming to 'the SU house on Mission Hill', Bill's rented one-bedroom building with its spacious downstairs living-room.

The only thing they could do was to find out what God had to say about their situation through their prayers and Bible studies. Up to 100 students were turning up at Mission Hill each week-day, sometimes staying all day. Here was a totally unplanned Bible School, with a nucleus of school and college students who proved their Christian commitment and leadership qualities by helping Bill with his meetings.

Sealed off from the outside world and from Nigeria by besieging forces, Bill and his friends had to become resourceful. Selling his remaining stock of books provided food for the first six months. As supplies became increasingly scarce, they relied on locally grown crops. The students helped Bill grow yams, tomatoes and okra in his garden.

After nine months of war, starvation became a serious problem. As the Nigerian armies gradually advanced on Biafra, more refugee camps sprang up to shelter the retreating population. 'Biafra was slowly being squeezed out of existence,' says Bill. 'It was slow because the Ibos were determined to resist as long as possible, believing that if they lost the war, they would all be massacred. So they just fought and fought and it took two and a half years for the Nigerian armies to win the war.'

The Ibos' determination was also reflected in Bill's students' determination to follow Christ at all costs: 'As more and more of this world's goods were taken away from us, the young people seemed to be on fire for the Lord, reaching out in evangelism and personal witness to their friends and relatives.'

Just as starvation was taking hold, the World Council of Churches and the Catholic organisation Caritas combined to send supplies to two islands off the West African coast. Finally a few planeloads of relief and medical supplies began to be flown into Biafra under cover of darkness to escape the Nigerian air force. There was no airport, but a new highway served as an airstrip. That highway was to be Biafra's lifeline for two years.

Distribution of the food was organised by the churches and the remaining missionaries like Bill. They agreed that the Protestants and Catholics would take charge of the entire cargo on alternate nights.

So every other night drivers took their empty lorries out to the airstrip to wait for the sounds in the darkness which indicated that a plane was on its way. Only when they were about to land did the planes briefly switch their lights on. This happened ten, fifteen or even twenty times a night.

Another constant battle was against corruption. 'When you have starving people in large numbers, the people handling the food always have enormous temptations to sell it or break into the stores and steal it for their own families.'

It became apparent that a number of lorry drivers were stopping off at their own village on the way to unload some supplies before driving on to their intended destination. The organisers were at their wits' end and asked Bill if he could supply a number of incorruptible young men who would travel with the drivers and be responsible for the load's security.

Bill was more than happy to oblige, and over 50 of his students helped hold the operation together over the next year. Much more food now got through to the most needy people in the camps and makeshift bush hospitals. As the needs increased, so Bill was asked for more young men and women who were strong enough Christians to resist temptation and oversee fair distribution.

He was impressed by his students' response. As Ibos, they could enter army camps and hospitals, where he, a foreigner, was refused entry.

People were going out in teams, sharing the love of Christ in refugee camps and with the wounded soldiers, who were coming back in ever-increasing numbers. Even if our students had to move to another part of Biafra with their families, they went

JOIN ME FOR LUNCH ON SUNDAY

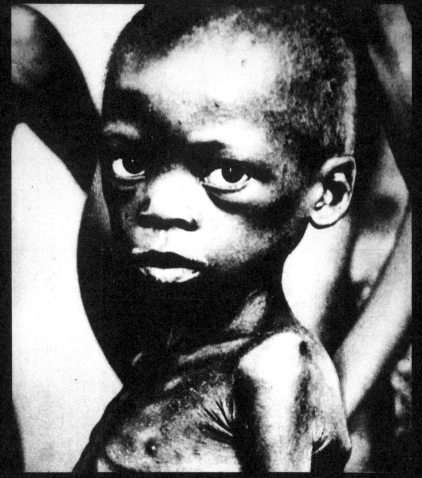

I can't offer you much, but perhaps you won't mind going a little hungry for just one day.

Remember that two-thirds of the world's people always feel hungry – and 12,000 of us die of starvation each day.

If you will join me for a sparse meal, then April 29th – TEAR Fund Sunday – is the date to plan for. On that day Christians will be getting together as families or in church fellowships to focus their prayers and attention on hungry and suffering people the world over.

TEAR Fund will use the money you save to bring help quickly and in the Name of Christ to those who need it most.

Please don't forget us.

TEAR FUND
Registered Name Relief Fund

19 Draycott Place, London SW3 2SJ

APRIL 29th IS TEAR FUND SUNDAY

as fired-up Christians and started fellowships similar to that which we had enjoyed at Mission Hill.

As well as these vibrant fellowships springing up all over Biafra (100 by the end of the war) evangelism continued at home on Mission Hill, too. Throughout the war, Bill and his young committee held a monthly guest service, to which many, despite being weak from starvation, walked from 10 or 20 miles away, often bringing unconverted friends.

They had such a zeal to go and win their friends for Christ that their own well-being just didn't seem to matter. It was a tremendous challenge to see the physical sacrifices they made under those conditions, because after a year we all realised we were experiencing semi-starvation to varying degrees.

The food kept coming in, but there was never enough for everybody. Sickness followed starvation, bringing a double threat to the Biafrans, especially in the refugee camps where Bill saw children just lying limply on the ground, in the process of starving to death. By the end of the war, starvation had claimed between two and three million lives.

At this time Bill received a message from SU headquarters. There was a new relief organisation called Tear Fund, which wondered if he had any needs. He promptly cabled back, 'Yes, we have *enormous* needs!' And so Bill became one of the first dozen recipients of a Tear Fund grant. Bill's right-hand man, Raymond, handled the Tear Fund money and used his discretion to select local families who had no idea how to feed the relatives who arrived on their thresholds after fleeing from the advancing Nigerian army. Bill personally housed several other students whose only other destination would have been a refugee camp. This open door policy qualified him to receive a weekly food ration of corn meal which, with hot water added, provided one meal a day.

The most frightening time was when bombing raids started. Sometimes Bill would go out in his car and just pick up the bodies, hoping some were only wounded. 'Everybody had to face up to the possibility of death at any time. Africans are very God-conscious, very aware that there is a God, there will be a judgement, and that therefore they must be ready to meet their God and give account of their lives.'

Consequently, when Bill and others delivered sacks of food to starving people in refugee camps, they found people who also had a deep spiritual hunger.

Those of us who knew and loved the Lord found we could quite naturally start talking about him. People would immediately leave the food and crowd around us, just to listen. As we started talking about the love of God, how he had sent Jesus Christ to die for our sins and was willing to forgive and give us a new life in Christ, many just wanted to give their lives to him in a wonderful way. It was quite extraordinary – I'd never seen anything like it.

This scene was repeated all over Biafra as Bill's students went out amongst their people. As a result, many people became Christians and, in Bill's words, 'knew a new sense of joy as they were starving to death'.

Such joy in the face of adversity was particularly evident in camps where Bill had been able to leave strong Christians in charge.

When you have hundreds and thousands of displaced people who are worried about their relatives and their futures, it's easy for fear to take hold, and I believe anxious people died much sooner. But I was convinced that in those camps where people were being taught from the Bible to trust in the Lord, that the food went much further! The difference between camps where the gospel was taught and where there weren't Christian leaders was quite marked.

What of the well-worn argument that a loving God would not allow people to suffer? Bill is in no doubt that the Biafrans knew the war had come as a result of political corruption and tribal in-fighting which the Ibos had borne for years: 'No-one blamed God.'

In the last nine months of the war, the Nigerian army finally overran Umuahia. As soon as the shells started exploding, Bill and his friends fled to the countryside.

In the last month before Biafra collapsed Bill caught malaria. Eventually he was taken to a hospital and then flown out.

Bill now believes that God engineered his exit on a stretcher:

We'd agreed that all the ex-patriates would be flown out by the Red Cross before Biafra finally collapsed, because three other missionaries who had surrendered to the advancing Nigerian forces had been lined up and shot, which caused an outcry in the West. But I was so close to my African brethren that I would still have found it exceedingly difficult to leave them.

A year after they married, Bill took his wife, Jan, to Nigeria for a month of ministry at Scripture Union camps. It gave Jan the opportunity to meet many of her husband's former students.

Going back reminded Bill of the many times that key scripture, 'Lo, I am with you always', had re-entered his mind.

It was not that I thought he would in any way make it easy for us or comfortable or even safer, but he was with us, and that assurance was so valuable and his presence so real at times of suffering. I think one would have to say we experienced his presence in a way that you don't normally in peaceful, comfortable times.

That very sense of God's presence often gave Bill the encouragement he needed, 'proof that I was in the right place, doing the right thing, and whatever happened, he was going to be in it with you'.

The Biafran experience taught Bill one great truth; that the physically hungry are spiritually hungry.

Whenever I see the faces of starving children and adults on the television now, as I saw every day in Biafra, I see the fear of death in those who haven't made their peace with God, who don't have the assurance that their sins are forgiven, and don't

know that if they die next week or next month they will go to
heaven to be with the Lord for ever.

Bill Roberts succeeded Ernest Oliver as Director of Tear Fund's
Overseas Evangelism and Education Department in 1986 where
he stayed until 1992, when he began working among international
students in the area around his Richmond church.

Disasters – whose fault?

In George Hoffman's words, Tear Fund was born out of disaster.

> In our case it was the famine in the Bihar region of India; the
> invasion of South Vietnam, and the civil upheaval of Jordan.
> And ever since, as the Bible predicts of the poor, it seems that
> disasters of one kind or another have been always with us . . .
> war, famine, earthquake and floods.
>   Over the years, like an action-replay of a series of nightmares,
> I can recall my own exposure, shock and horror on being
> involved in the human tragedies that follow in the wake of
> every disaster.

Tear Fund is increasingly seen by supporters as a channel for a rapid
response to disasters. As a result, every year a significant proportion
of Tear Fund's resources enable Christians on the spot to respond
immediately and effectively to the urgent needs around them.

But why do disasters occur? Tear Fund believe the Bible has an
explanation: sin on a worldwide scale. Stephen Rand, Tear Fund's
Communications Director, explains that an unharmonious, even
dangerous, environment is a result of the Fall, as surely as broken relationships with God and each other. Christians see natural
disasters as evidence of the deep effect of sin on the whole created
order, which groans as if in the pains of childbirth (Romans 8:22).

Sin often makes natural disasters worse. Poverty forces many
to live in unsafe locations, simply because they cannot afford to
move away. Some disasters are the direct result of greed and
exploitation.

But there is hope, in the fact of the gospel which sets people
free from sin. The gospel motivates people to care for the victims
of disaster and offers freedom to the oppressed, including those
oppressed by wealth and power; they can be freed to use their
riches for others.

'God has promised to restore the order he originally created, with
a new heaven and a new earth, where the trees clap their hands for
joy,' says Stephen.

But there are no easy answers as to why particular disasters occur.
Some may be quick to perceive God's judgement at work, but Jesus

himself was careful to make clear that hasty conclusions must be avoided: 'Do you think that these Galileans (who had been killed by the Roman authorities) were worse sinners than all the other Galileans because they suffered this way? I tell you, no! But unless you repent, you too will all perish.' (Luke 13:2–3)

One thing is clear: disasters offer unique opportunities and challenges to the Christian to demonstrate the reality of the gospel.

How relief grants are made

As soon as Tear Fund learns of a disaster, its Regional Manager for that continent will contact evangelical groups on the spot to find out how they are planning to respond. Together they draw up a budget to cover the cost of immediate relief work, which in turn is submitted to a rapidly convened meeting of Tear Fund's own in-house overseas grants committee.

Assuming Tear Fund has money available, it approves the funds and sends them as quickly as possible to its partners. Some relief partners, such as Philrads in the earthquake prone Philippines and EFICOR in India, have been given special emergency relief funds to ensure that money is available for an instant response.

After the immediate crisis, a report is sent back describing the use of the grant, and indicating if further relief assistance or longer-term rehabilitation and development work is needed.

Rapid response

The man with the job of co-ordinating a rapid response to disaster situations is Relief Manager Mike Wall. In keeping with Tear Fund's desire to help people to help themselves, Mike holds training workshops and study visits for overseas partners and churches to be able to respond effectively to disasters in their countries. For instance, he arranged for a group of Angolan pastors to visit Ethiopia to see how the Church was dealing with drought in that post-Communist war-torn country.

Training for disasters

In his 'disaster workshops', Mike and his colleagues instruct people in the skills and qualities vital for life and death situations. To back up his workshops he has just produced *Christian Perspectives on Disaster Management*, a resource manual which gives biblical precedents to disaster management, citing Joseph and the famine in Egypt, Nehemiah's dangerous rebuilding of Jerusalem, Paul's supervision of famine relief in Judea and other biblical material.

Bringing the problem up to date, national Christians and other experts advise on the skills necessary in a life and death situation.

These include time management, leadership, logistics and 'preparedness planning', which in the case of, say, an earthquake, could involve evacuation procedures. Essential qualities are flexibility and a sense of humour under stress!

Proof of the effectiveness of training local leaders in evacuation procedures was seen when he visited Nicaragua. 'The city of Rama had been flooded to the point that only the cross on top of the church steeple was visible, yet the whole town had been evacuated before the floods during heavy rain, because they had drawn up an evacuation plan and everyone knew where to go.'

The manual also tells readers how to conduct a feeding programme and build houses which are safe against earthquakes.

As a former barrister, Mike is used to keeping a cool head and thinking on his feet. Before joining Tear Fund he spent a year in the Inner Temple and then moved to a Community Law Centre in west London where he became involved in campaigning against poor housing and racial violence.

With Tear Fund he went to Sudan where he managed a refugee project, and experienced rapid evacuation himself along with other Westerners after the well-publicised kidnap of a Tear Fund nurse, Heather Sinclair. Back in Britain, he spent a year as a Crown Prosecutor before studying for a term at Oxford's Refugee Studies Programme. Then he returned to Tear Fund as Relief Manager.

The uniqueness of Tear Fund's role in ministering to the whole person was illustrated for Mike at a disaster workshop for pastors

in Mozambique. During a field trip which took place halfway through
the workshop they were sent out with a check list of questions to find
out about other groups' relief projects.

When they came to a project run by a secular group, they asked
the usual question, 'How is your church involved?'

'The church has never been to this place', they were told.

Realising they were face to face with a totally unevangelised
village, the pastors began to preach! Soon they attracted a crowd
of 400 to hear the good news of Jesus Christ. They were found in
the middle of a huge throng of people gathered round a fire. After
hearing that idols should not be worshipped, everyone was bringing
their fetishes to destroy in the fire.

'This was an example of how even when you're doing something
dry and technical, you can't restrain the Holy Spirit from building
God's Kingdom,' says Mike.

Anatomy of a disaster

Tear Fund is ready to respond to every phone call, telex or fax
alerting it to a disaster. Within hours funds will be on the way to
the trouble spot. The diagram on the following page from *3rd Track*,
Tear Fund's youth magazine, shows exactly how it all works.

ISSUE 13:4

3RD TRACK

FACT TRACK
DISASTER RELIEF

Rapid Relief

When disaster strikes, Tear Fund aims to respond as quickly as possible. Here's what happens:

COUNTDOWN

- News of disaster breaks. On TV; in the newspapers; by fax from the United Nations.

- Tear Fund contacts partner in country where disaster has occurred. Do they need any help?

- Partner goes to the disaster site to see what help is needed.

- Help is asked for.

- Tear Fund's Overseas Committee meet immediately and decide what support to send.

- Support is sent. Money can be transferred straight away. Other things may take longer.

- Relief work starts.

- Partner reports on exactly what's been done and how well it's worked.

- More help may be needed to help communities get back to normal life.

CURRENT CASE

12th December 1992 An earthquake (7.5 Richter scale) occurred in the Sawu sea, south of Flores Island, Indonesia.

12th - 14th December Faxes received from UN Dept of Humanitarian Affairs giving information relating to the disaster and relief action being taken. Story reported in national newspapers.

14th December Mike Wall, Tear Fund's Relief Manager faxed partners, YUSI, to ask if assistance was needed.

16th December Partner sent report of the situation and asked for money to buy blankets, tents, medicines, kerosene lamps and drinking water.

17th December Tear Fund's Overseas Grants Committee considered the request and approved a grant of £15,541.42. Money sent to YUSI by bank transfer. YUSI started relief work.

At time of going to press:
Relief Operation underway.

Indonesia Death Toll climbs to 1,600

Maumere, Indonesia
Almost 1,600 bodies have been found after an earthquake and huge tidal waves turned parts of Indonesia's 'Isle of Flowers' into a cemetery. On the outskirts of the town of Maumere, survivors said tidal waves swamped their fishing village three times and swept many of the hamlet's 2,000 residents away.
(Independent 15:12:92)

PLEASE TRANSMIT ON FAX

TO: Mr Laban, Projects Director, YUSI
FROM: Mike Wall, Relief Manager, Tear Fund

We were concerned to hear of the recent earthquake affecting the island of Flores. Please contact us immediately if we can assist in any way with a grant or commodities for relief work amongst the affected population or with longer term needs arising from the disaster.

Dear Mr Wall,

Thank you for your compassionate fax. The total number of people killed in this horrible disaster is 2,484 and this number will increase gradually because it excludes those wiped out by Tsunami* tidal waves. Can you imagine what a horrific and tragic situation when a huge Tsunami (twenty-five metres high) came and caught them suddenly and wiped them out from the land into the ocean to disappear.
In Maumere, 40,000 people have fled the rubble of their destroyed homes and sleep in open fields outside the city.
The relief needs are blankets, tents, medicine, kerosene lamps and drinking water.

David Laban, YUSI (16.12.92)

*Tsunami = tidal wave caused by an earthquake on the sea bed.

CHAPTER SIX

BANGLADESH:
LOVE NEVER GIVES UP

O n his way home from Australia in October 1973, where he had given a concert performance in the new Sydney Opera House, Cliff Richard joined Bill Latham and George Hoffman in Bangladesh. Formerly East Pakistan, it was suffering from the combined catastrophes of civil war and a cyclone.

Visiting the Bihari refugee camps in the capital, Dhaka, provided an experience that led him to say afterwards, 'I'll never be the same again.'

Some of the things he saw remained vivid in his mind over a decade later – watching an 18-month-old baby die of starvation because his parents could not afford to feed him; recoiling in horror at another tiny baby covered in sores and scabs, but then instinctively grabbing hold of him when someone accidentally trod on his fingers. The baby hugged him, and this became, in Bill Latham's words, 'a moment of touching when he got over all the fear and the taboos of it all. He often talks of that little encounter and has a large framed picture in his bedroom of him holding that child'.

Other recollections were less painful – a patient who was so proud of a bullet embedded in his side that he insisted everyone must feel it; the indefatigable cheerfulness of the occupants of a children's ward, many of whom were dreadfully injured or burned; and above all the love and patience of the nurses tending the sick.

One of those nurses was Liz Hutchison, now Liz Wilkinson. Working for the BMMF, (the Bible and Medical Missionary Fellowship – now Interserve) and funded by Tear Fund. She left Britain in January 1973 to work in a large orthopaedic hospital in Dhaka, and spent her first six weeks overseas treating young amputees and paralytics, mainly wounded soldiers.

At the request of the Southern Baptist Missionary Society, she went to help set up a clinic for inmates of a refugee camp. As she was trained in general and paediatric nursing, she specialised in treating the children, feeding, clothing, washing and giving them medicine. There was also a smallpox epidemic when she arrived, so she and many others plunged into a mass vaccination programme, which also included vaccinating against measles, mumps, whooping

cough and diphtheria. Since that time in Bangladesh, smallpox has
been eradicated, thanks mainly to the work of the World Health
Organisation, with whom Liz and
her colleagues co-operated.

By the time Cliff visited, Liz
was preparing to come home because the project was function-
ing smoothly. Totally absorbed
by her work, Liz was unaware
of the impact it made on Cliff.

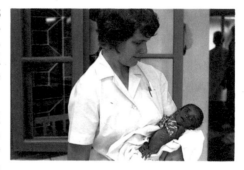

He and George Hoffman and
Bill Latham came out to the
house where I lived with other
Tear Fund personnel and we
went out to the camp. He followed my routine of picking up
the children from a particular
area where they'd congregated,
taking them to the clinic where
we bathed and fed them, and
then visiting the smaller clinics within the camp where they
delivered babies and gave general medical treatment.

Cliff and I talked a lot during the day and in the evenings
he would come back and have a meal with us. Then the group
of us would sing and talk together.

It was during one of those gentle, reflective conversations, that Cliff
said to Liz, 'You know, what I have seen today makes me feel as
though I want to give it all up and come out here and work.'

Liz turned to him and said, very quietly, 'Can you give an injection
or put a person on a drip?'

'No, I'd be horrified', Cliff replied.

'Well, you go back home and raise money for us to do it,' Liz
said. 'That's what you can do and this is what we do. That's what
it's all about.

Bill remembers it as a draining time.

I'd been to Africa, but Asia is another experience. There are
so many people and the activity is so frantic. It was hot, it
was humid – and there were long days just traipsing around
in mud and muck – it was a horrendous time.

If Cliff needed any convincing of the value of Tear Fund's
work, this was it.

Meeting the nurses was an important part of the experience, according to Bill. 'They were there because that's where they felt led by God, magnificent people who were just the embodiment of Christ's teaching, demonstrating his love.'

Cliff himself paid full tribute to the dedication of the nurses, admitting that two hours in the camp felt like five hours. 'They go through a lot of emotional traumas. So, if for nothing else, I felt it was good to be there because the nurses did need the boost of having fellowship and contact with us all. For them, every day is a lifetime.'

The extent of extreme poverty and degradation was something Cliff had never seen before. Liz remembers the impact of her first sight of relief work. 'We'd been briefed about the climate and suitable clothing for a Muslim culture, but nothing could prepare us for the poverty, the starvation and the death.'

Whereas death in the West is very private and shrouded in genteel rituals, Liz, an experienced nurse, still had to get accustomed to the starkness of death on the streets – bodies in the road which had to be loaded into lorries every day.

Some of the refugees lived in huge sewage pipes, some in derelict buildings, some in shanty houses, protected by whatever bits of coconut matting or plastic they could find. Liz recalls that:

> There was no sanitation. Water had to be collected from stand-pipes. Sometimes I wondered what I was doing as a nurse. I felt I should have been working in agriculture. What's the point of making people better if they can't feed themselves?

Sadly, the troubles in Bangladesh were not over. In 1974 Liz Wilkinson returned to help with the after-effects of severe flooding, working again with refugees whose village homes had been swept away.

It was in November 1970 that the greater part of Bangladesh (or East Pakistan as it was then called) was struck by one of the most lethal tidal waves ever known in the area. Tear Fund's Financial Administrator of the time, Charles Phillimore, was able to establish links with the Evangelical Fellowship of India and International Christian Fellowship, through whom emergency relief supplies were channelled to help the thousands made homeless by this disaster.

But as nurse Liz Wilkinson pointed out, 'It's a whole series of problems which need addressing together. You've got to give people spiritual food and physical food.'

This has been the challenge facing HEED Bangladesh, the initials

The Poverty Chain
Poster Presentation

A thousand million of the world's population are trapped in a chain of poverty.
They struggle for survival in countries that are desperately poor.
Sometimes these countries are called the "Third World" — as opposed to the "First World" of the industrial western nations and the "Second World" of the communist countries.
More often they are referred to as the "developing" countries ... of the southern hemisphere ... as this map shows.
They struggle for survival — victims of an unfair trading system — often heavily in debt which further retards their economic growth.
The gap between the rich world and the world of those caught in the poverty gap is relentlessly widening year by year.

TEAR FUND
11 Station Road Teddington
Middx TW11 9AA

He has sent me to proclaim freedom ^{Luke 4:18}

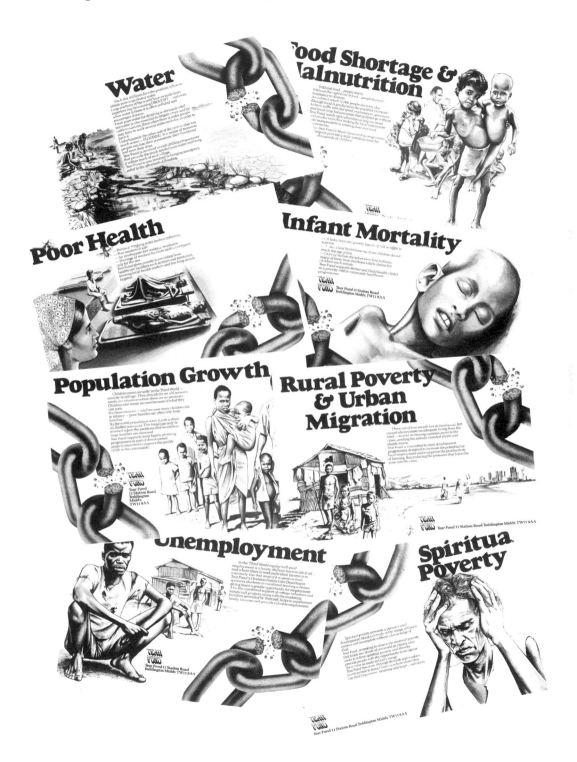

standing for Health, Education and Economic Development, which
Tear Fund was instrumental in launching with five other Christian
organisations in October 1974.

By 1984 three main projects had grown up: the Dhaka camps
project, the Kamalganj rural development project and the Dacope
Thana health services project. In all, Tear Fund had allocated more
than £1 million in development grants over that first ten years, as
well as the services of more than 50 Tear Fund workers, several of
whom chose to serve at least eight years in Bangladesh.

Tearcraft comes winging in

A hasty decision to make the maximum use of a Tear Fund relief
plane saw the birth of Tearcraft, the Tear Fund operation specialising in selling Third World craft products. Known to thousands
through its colourful catalogue picturing all sorts of desirable items
from plant holders to jewellery, Tearcraft traces its origins back to
the 1974 Bangladesh flood disaster.

Tear Fund chartered a plane to send its medical and other relief
supplies to Bangladesh. Instead of returning empty, the plane
was loaded with several tons of jute handicraft products for sale
in Britain. The success of this venture opened the way for the
creation of Tearcraft in 1975, which naturally included plenty of
HEED Handicrafts.

Cliff and Tear Fund

Cliff Richard's purpose in visiting Bangladesh was to help
make a Tear Fund film-strip,
Love never gives up, the first
of several audio-visuals in which
he featured, including two highly
popular films, *Cliff in Kenya* and
It's a Small World. These in turn
inspired him to write songs based
on his response to what he saw.

And, following Liz Wilkinson's
advice, it is Cliff's singing which
has done more than anything
else to identify him with Tear
Fund. Every two or three years
since 1969, he has set aside time
from his regular engagements to
fit in a gospel concert tour which
has taken him to large and small
venues all round the country.

After he became a Christian in 1965, Cliff attended the same Anglican church in Finchley as his friend Bill Latham and David Winter, who were both lay readers. David, then editor of *Crusade* magazine, asked Cliff if he would take part in a fund-raising concert for a small outfit called Tear Fund. 'I don't think either of us had any indication at that time that it would play such a major role in out lives,' says Bill Latham. 'Help, Hope and Hallelujah!', was the exuberant title of Cliff's first concerts in 1969, which were to be the forerunners of many more.

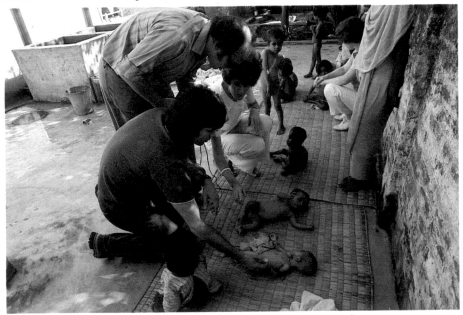

Bill believes that this introduction to the work of Tear Fund made Cliff realise he 'needed this sort of outlet to express his concern for those in need. With hindsight he saw it as the perfect opportunity for someone like him with responsibility and resources'.

But Cliff doesn't just raise money from other people for Tear Fund; he himself gets involved as a roving ambassador. Over the years he has visited seven countries for Tear Fund, spontaneously making friends and maintaining contacts where he can. Looking back, Cliff admits that working for Tear Fund was indeed hard work. 'I could never say I really enjoyed myself, and yet when you balance it out I wouldn't have missed it for anything.'

Although he had gone through traumatic experiences every day in places like Bangladesh or Sudan, he had rich memories of happy evenings laughing over a meal with Bill, Tony Neeves and George Hoffman. 'We had wonderful times together – not always *enjoyable* times, but wonderful times.'

Working for Tear Fund certainly helped change Cliff's outlook. 'George taught me that the problems of this world will always continue and those of us that say we're Christian must continue to love and therefore dedicate and commit ourselves to the needy.'

Pauline Hoffman also influenced Cliff. 'During a meal at their house, I was thinking about my fame and my success – and I had lots of both, when Pauline quoted, "To whom much is given, you know, much is expected in return." It wasn't easy, but I've tried to live up to that!'

Tear Fund has never been blatant about its association with Cliff, which may explain the success of the relationship. Cliff has been able to slip quietly into countries and meet Tear Fund partners and personnel in their workplaces and sympathise with the challenges they face, as he first did in Bangladesh.

At the press launch of his video, *Compassion has the Heart*, in October 1992, representatives of national newspapers were heard asking, 'What is the Tear Fund?'

'Tear Fund hasn't been concerned to go to the media, because that's not where it gets its support,' explains Bill Latham, who left Tear Fund to manage the growing volume of Cliff's Christian work. 'Its target is the person in the pew. And look at the size of its income – does it need to go to the public?'

Over the years, Cliff's gospel concerts have directly raised £500,000 for the work of Tear Fund, but the indirect results of his involvements are incalculable. The success of Cliff's role was recognised by his appointment as Vice President in 1984. Twenty-five years is a long time to sustain the level of involvement and support which he has shown, though he would be the first to agree that he is only one of hundreds and thousands of people who have shown equal commitment to the work of Tear Fund.

Bill Latham reminisced in a *Tear Times* article in 1979 . . .

I guess some of the most memorable concerts with Cliff were in India and Bangladesh. No band – just Cliff and a guitar – and some dodgy amplification. But the reception could not have been more enthusiastic. Vijayan Pavamani, that lovely Christian brother and church leader from Calcutta, who was the principal speaker at Tear Fund's recent series of anniversary meetings around Britain, described those concerts as 'undoubtedly the most significant evangelism that has taken place in Calcutta over recent years'. A similar concert in a hotel lounge in Dhaka saw probably the most unlikely audience of all – a mixture of high-ranking military and government leaders, most of them Muslim or Hindu. Diplomatically, it was magnificent for Tear Fund's operations in Bangladesh, spiritually it was a unique opportunity. One Christian Bengali, a senior radio executive, who was broadcasting the concerts to literally tens of millions of Bangladeshis in villages through the land, was so moved by the witness of his programme that he broke down and wept on Cliff's shoulder.

HEALTH

Healing the sick is a vital part of demonstrating the gospel today – as it was for Jesus. The emphasis within Tear Fund's extensive involvement in healthcare is on preventive and community health, providing basic healthcare for all. Immunisation, health education, mother and child clinics – all are important weapons in the battle against disease.

Two pounds profit a day is riches in the poor village of Kamarkhola in Dacope, southern Bangladesh. This is what Kalpona and her husband Durgapada earn three days a week when Durgapada sells their home-grown vegetables at market. Before Kalpona went on a HEED agricultural course, Durgapada was a day labourer working for local landlords in his own and neighbouring villages.

Once Kalpona had learnt how to use balanced doses of chemical fertiliser on their land along with cow dung and compost, she suggested to her husband that they cultivate their land intensively instead of working hard for others for low wages. Durgapada, who had also received some training from HEED, agreed, and now they have enough pumpkins, chillies, gourds, sweet pumpkins, ladies' fingers (okra), winter vegetables (cauliflower, cabbage), bridal (aubergine) and various leafy vegetables to feed their family and earn money by selling them throughout the year. The family is an example in their village that hard toil on even a small plot of land can give a family enough food to survive.

Food

More people have died as a consequence of hunger in the past five years than have been killed in all the wars, revolutions and murders in the past 150 years.

Spending

Most families in poor countries spend 80–90 per cent of their income on food, compared with 25 30 per cent for families in Western Europe.

Urban ministry

Increasingly the growing population of the world is concentrating in urban areas where unemployment, inadequate housing and breakdown of the family and social structures cause severe problems for the poor. Tear Fund is working with Christian partners seeking to express the relevance of the gospel in often desperate situations, particularly focussing on the needs of abandoned and orphaned children.

Living off the land

– Most people in the Third World live directly off the land – as many as 90 per cent in Nepal, Rwanda and Burundi.
– Women do 80 per cent of the work on the land.
– Chronic malnutrition is more widespread than famine and is on the increase among developing countries.
– Total world grain production is no longer keeping pace with rapid population growth.
– Half the trees which are felled worldwide are not cut down by large corporations but by small farmers fighting for the survival of their families.

Tear Fund enables its Christian partners to work with poor farmers in sustainable development, helping to defend and renew the environment while providing for current needs.

Rural development

Wherever possible, Tear Fund supports integrated programmes, involving healthcare, nutrition, food production, water supply – all provided through Christian partners who are working in a context of holistic mission and evangelism.

Weapons

The money spent on weapons on the world in one hour is the amount needed to give the injections that would stop 3.5 million children dying every year from infectious diseases.

CHAPTER SEVEN

ETHIOPIA: A FUTURE AND A HOPE

'The people went wild, jumping the fence and looking down the hole and shaking our hands.'

So reported Tear Fund's drilling engineers Peter Ball and Mick Williams after they first struck water in Ethiopia in spring 1974.

For the women of that village, the well meant the end of trekking five miles with heavy water pots to a typhoid-contaminated, stinking water-hole. 'They just stood there with their hands in front of their mouths, unbelieving and in bewilderment.'

Rev Pat Goodland, a member of Tear Fund's Main Committee, accompanied the rig with a team. Out of the trip came one of Tear Fund's early soundstrips, a 15-minute documentary entitled *In Search of Water*. It conveyed the desperate needs of the people in Wollo and Tigre provinces, as well as describing how God overruled in airfreighting a £56,000 drilling rig to the drought regions.

The fact that money had been raised in the first place for the rig was due, Pat believes, to the heightened public awareness of the two-year Ethiopian drought and famine following a television broadcast by Jonathan Dimbleby. 'Three-quarters of a million people had died and the world had simply never seen such devastating pictures.'

Providing a well-drilling rig and truck was Tear Fund's biggest project to date, and its supporters provided £30,000; the rest came from a German relief charity, Christoffel-Blinden Mission.

Pat, the minister of Stanmore Baptist Church, had added Tear Fund to his responsibilities as a result of friendship with George Hoffman and was involved in its first seven years of life.

The well-drilling project was typical of Tear Fund's early days, when raw enthusiasm was in greater evidence than experience. The request for a drilling rig had come in October 1973 from SIM, the Society of International Missionaries, then known as the Sudan Interior Mission.

As Pat was chaplain to the headquarters of RAF Strike Command, his fellow Tear Fund committee members turned to him: 'You're RAF – can't you organise something?'

So Pat recruited two Christian RAF officers, Squadron Leaders Mike Cole and Dick Bell, a test pilot, and engineer Ernie Elliman from his congregation. The RAF was very helpful, but regulations required that a civil cargo aircraft be used. In the end Pat tracked down two Hercules transports of Alaska Airways. The rig mast was flown out from Gatwick and the main rig from Southend Airport. By letting down the tyres on the truck they got the rig into the plane with an inch to spare. Packed around and under the rig was £1,700 worth of blankets, tents and camp beds.

There were other minor miracles on the way. Pat recalls a British engineer working for Ethiopian Airways who happened to be on hand at Addis Ababa when they were trying to reassemble the rig.

> We'd lost a couple of nuts and bolts, and this man loaned us his equipment to get the rig together again. It was a miracle we ever got out of Addis Ababa because the government was so volatile – every day officials changed their minds about letting us out of the airport. We had just three weeks to take out the rig and try it out on site, so we were very relieved when they let us go after five days with a minute to spare before they closed the government offices for a long weekend. Later, on the way back to Addis, we stopped a mere three inches from an Ethiopian who slipped and fell in front of our vehicle.

They headed for Alamata, the main area of devastation. The Ethiopian governor of Wollo, a Moslem, greeted the team courteously and enthusiastically. He also paid them an extraordinary compliment: 'We've been asking the United Nations for rigs for a long time – we want eight, really. But I know why you got through – you're Jesus' men, aren't you?'

Encouraged by this testament to their faith, they tried to set up

the rig, only to realise that logistics in the Third World were quite
different from the society they had left behind. Pat needed piping
for the rig, which took much longer to reach them than they had
hoped. 'I had to take the initiative and spend money out there just
to get the job done properly. George was cross with me because I
spent more money than I should have done, but we wouldn't have
got the job done if we hadn't.'

Tear Times carried a report of the events following their arrival
by Mike Cole and Dick Bell:

> To British eyes, straight from north London, the sights of
> human suffering were horrific. Children of six to eight were
> little more than living skeletons and the eyes of these little
> ones looked with some expectancy into our faces. After all,
> we must be something to do with the missionaries – so we
> must be worthy of trust. One night we gave out the Tear
> Fund blankets. The people kissed our feet, legs and knees
> – total gratitude for so very little. Our cardboard ration
> boxes became cradles for newborn babies and the empty tins
> would be treasures for the rest of their lives. We had to
> remind ourselves that these people, so poor, full of insects
> and weeping sores, are also those for whom Jesus came to
> give fullness of life.

Suffering was not confined to the Ethiopians. Stress of a different
sort was being experienced by the two British Tear Fund nurses,
Heather Bobbersmien and Judith Crowe, who were running the
emergency clinic at Alamata. In a week these two girls in their
twenties were making more medical decisions than a doctor would
have to make in a year. When the team arrived, the men looked
after the camp for two days while the nurses rested for the first
time in months. 'You've saved us from having nervous breakdowns,'
Pat was told.

The need for a fresh water supply could not be exaggerated: 'We
saw people at the bottom of their wells scooping up mud from among
the rats and filth and squeezing out a few drops of water,' reported
Mike and Dick.

> As the well got into operation, it was humbling to see how
> grateful these people were – not in the wishy-washy way we
> thank people at home, but completely from within them. In
> their eyes you could see them saying thank you, not out of
> awkwardness and custom, but out of sheer appreciation of a
> clean water supply.

An even more touching response came when the village chief

walked into the mission station 12 miles away to ask for a teacher.

> . . . His villagers wanted to learn our way from the Bible. This is in a village which would have stopped any attempt at trying to give them a Bible teacher a few months before. Now there is a full-time teacher in that village and the well is producing water for 1,500 people a day.

Mission accomplished, Pat's team handed over the task to engineers Peter Ball and Mick Williams, who used the rig to sink 90 per cent of all new wells in Ethiopia over a four-month period in the autumn of 1974. The operation started slowly and painfully, but soon reached the point where seven holes were drilled in seven weeks. When a Canadian engineer eventually succeeded them, he created 168 wells.

Sadly, Pat remembers the work coming to an end when the Communist government commandeered the truck as a personnel carrier for their troops, although Tear Fund was to undertake numerous other projects in Ethiopia.

For your gifts and prayers – thank you!
The response of Tear Fund's supporters to the Ethiopian drought put them on the map, as far as SIM was concerned. Don Stilwell,

their co-ordinator for relief and rehabilitation in Ethiopia, wrote his
thanks to the Tear Fund offices:

> Only a few months ago Tear Fund was little more than a name
> to me. I could not have dreamed at that time that the largest
> single aid project so far of our massive Relief and Rehabilitation
> effort would come largely through the generous participation of
> Tear Fund.
>
> It is humbling to note that this generous response on the part
> of Tear Fund and its donors comes at a time when Britain is
> suffering under some of the severest economic stress of recent
> years. We can only imagine all the sacrifice this represents.
>
> The Lord has seen fit to use this national disaster to open the
> hearts and minds of many to the gospel. This is taking place in
> places which have traditionally been unresponsive . . .

Ten years later in October 1984, it took another moving BBC
broadcast, this time by Michael Buerk, to alert the world to
another Ethiopian famine. A new generation of givers flocked
to buy the Band Aid record and watch the Live Aid pop concert, inspired by singer Bob Geldof, where pop stars gave their
services free.

John Capon, then editor of *Tear Times*, and Stephen Rand, made
their own visit to Ethiopia in 1984. Following in the footsteps of
Pat Goodland, they flew up to Alamata in a small plane only to
be stranded when the plane was grounded in the wake of a rebel
attack on a nearby food convoy. 'To our dying days, Stephen and
I will remember the time we had to wait at that airstrip with
nothing more than the clothes we stood up in,' says John. 'That
experience may not register very high on the Richter scale with
hardened journalists or commandos, but we were neither and it was
very frightening!'

On the streets of Alamata, they were confronted with the suffering. In abject poverty, people were dying in public. The difference
between seeing such scenes on television and in the flesh, John
found, was that he now had 360 degree vision: 'You can see all
around you and smell the death and squalor.'

Once at their destination of Asmara, Ethiopia's second city and
capital of Eritrea before it became a separate nation, they visited
the grain distribution programme run by the Kale Heywet (Word
of Life) Church, one of Tear Fund's Ethiopian partners. They
saw shuffling queues waiting for their rations of grain, people
surging forward when the word went round that there might
not be enough to go around, and the pain of having to turn
some away.

They also visited Decamare in Eritrea, where the church ran a thriving school and orphanage for 50 boys. John wrote,

> The lively exuberance of the children is in sharp contrast to the shy, almost apologetic group of needy families sitting quietly in the corner of the school compound waiting for their name to be called to come forward and receive their grain allocation. They acknowledge receipt of the grain by putting their fingerprints on the record sheet. They then spread out their shawls to receive the grain, making sure that none goes astray, and move away clutching their precious cargo.

At the beginning of 1991, every indication was that Ethiopia was heading for a famine worse than that of 1984. Civil war combined with drought meant that 4.28 million people, nearly half of them in Eritrea in the north, would require food.

Once again, the Kale Heywet Church organised an ambitious famine relief programme to distribute nearly 8,000 tons of grain to 34,000 people in Asmara and Decamare. Tear Fund picked up the bill of £83,300, allocating a further £136,000 to the church's water, agriculture and reforestation programmes.

In this devastating crisis, there were reports that many were looking to the Church for answers – spiritual as well as physical. Hundreds turned to Christ, and the churches are overflowing.

This was a significant consolation in the midst of one national disaster after another. But the development has continued, with Tear Fund helping improve the lot of many Ethiopians through their partners over the last two decades, and despite development being what John Capon calls, 'a messy, thankless, on-going job – you just have to keep going'.

At last the civil war has come to an end in 1993 and Eritrea has been recognised as an independent country. Mike Webb, editor of *Tear Times* visited Asmara and Decamare again and produced a simple news video *New Hope for Eritrea* showing clearly the optimism for the future felt by the new nation and shared by the Church that could see new challenges and opportunities ahead.

Dr Mulatu Baffa has been committed to helping the poor in Ethiopia for the last 30 years. He is General Secretary of Tear Fund's Ethiopian partner, the Kale Heywet Church and since 1984 has been director of its programme to train church leaders in running their own small development programmes.

Naturally he has been grateful for the relief aid channelled into his country, but knows it is not the long-term answer. 'Ethiopia will take years of patient and laborious care to recover, but even now we can see signs of real hope.'

A thoroughly biblical response
Between preaching the gospel and supporting their churches, Paul and the early disciples of Jesus ensured that their faith was proved by works.

When a severe famine hit the Mediterranean region, and Judea in particular, in the early first century, the Church was ready. The famine had already been predicted by a prophetic message at the Antioch church, and the local believers used the existing church structure at home and in Jerusalem as a mechanism for collecting, transferring and distributing funds. Gifts given by the congregation were sent via Paul and Barnabas to the Judean elders (Acts 11:27–30, 2 Corinthians 9:12–14).

Some years later, Paul organised a similar effort, collecting funds from as far away as Macedonia and Achaia. (1 Corinthians 16:1–4, 2 Corinthians 8–9, Romans 15:25–28) Paul closely monitored the progress and encouraged giving when enthusiasm lagged. (2 Corinthians 8:10–12)

CHAPTER EIGHT

THE PHILIPPINES: BROKEN IMAGE

Think of the Philippines, and most people immediately recall Imelda Marcos' 1,000 pair of shoes. Even to Western eyes accustomed to conspicuous consumption, it was a shocking discovery in a land where many children went barefoot.

The discovery was made at the height of the 'People Power' revolution in 1986. As the deposed President Ferdinand Marcos and his wife, Imelda, boarded a chartered plane to escape the people's anger, the mob burst into the state palace. Amongst other imported luxuries they found row after row of Imelda's shoes, which included her famous disco dancing shoes with the flashing lights in the heels, which must have made frequent outings to Manila's exclusive night-clubs.

Less savoury aspects of Philippines' night life were recorded by a Tear Fund video crew three years later, showing child prostitution for the benefit of foreign servicemen as one product of a small, poor nation's exposure to a superpower. According to the *Manila Chronicle*, the Philippines has the highest number of street children

in South-east Asia – about 1.2 million. In Manila, up to 750,000 homeless children roam the streets.

This was one of many aspects of life in the Philippines which deeply affected singer Garth Hewitt, mime artist J Geoffrey Stevenson and poet Stewart Henderson when they joined forces with Stephen Rand of Tear Fund, film director John Muggleton and stage designer John Renfrew to create a video and gather material for a nationwide tour. *Broken Image* was the name chosen because, if people are made in God's image as the Bible says, that image has been broken by poverty and injustice in a nation like the Philippines: broken, but not destroyed. For the team also wanted to illustrate the resilience, hope and positive values of the people, and help break the image of the poor as helpless victims.

Sugar with a sour after-taste

American colonisation of the Philippines from 1898–1938 meant that sugar, already introduced by a British merchant in 1856, now became the islands' chief export at the expense of textile and agricultural industries. Demand by the American soft drinks industry enriched President Marcos and the sugar producers – until the diet-conscious 70s saw the US soft drinks industry switch to sugar substitutes. Almost overnight the demand for cane sugar slumped, leaving large areas of fertile land lying idle; and 250,000 people were unemployed, with 156,000 children suffering from malnutrition.

The search for work leads many into the cities. The *Broken Image* team followed one woman's precarious journey home in Surigao City to an area of houses rising on stilts out of a tidal swamp and linked by wooden planks. They were all squatters; although the woman had lived there for ten years, they had no rights to the land on which they built their homes. The damp heat of the swamp, stench of rubbish and lack of sanitation mercifully could not be conveyed on the video, but this was where this woman and her husband had decided to build their Christian marriage. Stewart Henderson conveyed a lot by mopping his brow and remarking, 'To call the situation unpromising would be an understatement.'

Nonetheless, the family had created a simple but lovingly kept home with bamboo floors and a Christian text hanging on the wall.

On Sundays they formed part of the 400-strong General Baptist Church led by Pepito Lapaz, who had already seen his church wrecked by a typhoon in 1984.

'Pastor, we only eat once a day and have five children.'

This remark made Pastor Agapito Castil think of Jesus feeding the five thousand; as a result he spent much of his day bent double, ankle-deep in a rice field, working alongside his flock to feed them.

At the end of the day they go from the rice field to a prayer meeting, to pray for both their rice harvest and a spiritual harvest, for their neighbours to know new life in Christ.

The field was provided by Philrads to enable his church to work together to improve their very basic living standards. Even here there was injustice to be found. When the landowner, a Filipino resident in the United States, heard that the project was planning to provide a pump so that the field could be irrigated and a second crop gained each year, he immediately doubled the rent. But for Agapito, the field still represents comparative prosperity for his church members: 'I saw the need; if we had land to farm and to plant rice, then there could be rice for the whole family.'

The image was also being restored on Smoky Mountain, Manila's municipal rubbish dump, which is home to 4,000 families. Constantly smoking from the fires below, Smoky Mountain has hidden troosurcs, both in terms of the rubbish which its residents sell for recycling and in spiritual terms; there are now five churches there, a sudden growth in the last few years.

One man, Pastor Antonio Senora, who founded his church there 17 years ago, has paid a steep price for remaining on Smoky Mountain, which he sees as God's call on his life. His daughter died from TB, which, along with diarrhoea and asthma, is rife on Smoky Mountain.

But the Tear Fund team, picking their way through mountains of rubbish and filth, could not get over the people's dignity and

Were you there, standing with George Hoffman and Tony Neeves, weeping over the capital city of the Philippines on Tear Fund Sunday, 1978?

Do you remember George's voice on the soundstrip – heavy and almost breaking with grief?

His words – and those pictures – pierced me with a sense of compassion, coupled with a horror that we are guilty of acquiescing in allowing our fellow men to exist in terrible conditions, through our inactivity on their behalf.

I have never been able to forget George's haunting words: 'In front of me is a huge mountain of debris . . . a great heap of garbage which reaches up to the sky. The stench from burning rubbish is choking – quite apart from the overwhelming smell of the putrid matter . . .'

His voice slowed and my heart went cold: 'On the edge of this tip are hundreds of little shacks and huts, literally clinging to that rubbish and reaching down to the sea . . .'

(Tear Times, Autumn 1982)

civilised behaviour: 'Their humanity shines through . . . these are people made in God's image.'

The people have 'shifts' for scavenging. One young man seen setting off for the night shift was Beltran Banzuelo, a former government employee who lost his job after the People's Revolution. Hook in hand and basket on shoulder, he wades into the mess, immediately finding items which he flicks skilfully over his shoulder into his basket.

When the night shift is over, Beltran finds time during the day to work for Pastor Senora, for since scavenging on Smoky Mountain, Beltran has become a Christian through Pastor Senora's church.

The product might be rubbish, but the money Beltran earns supports his extended family of seven and pays for his sister's teacher training course. He hopes she will then support the family while he goes to Bible College to train as a pastor. When Stephen Rand revisited Beltran in 1992, the generosity of some Tear Fund supporters had enabled him to restart his education.

Education is escape

'Wherever we went in the Philippines, we realised the people are working hard not just for themselves, but to invest in their children's future,' said Stewart Henderson.

In the fresh air of the seashore, the Tear Fund team found a fishing village, Nueva Sevilla, whose inhabitants knew a different sort of poverty, but the same ambitions. Here the size of the catch brought in by the fishermen at dawn to be sold by their wives at market determined the families' day-to-day survival.

With foreign vessels using dynamite to plunder their fish stocks a few miles off-shore, the Filipino fishermen they interviewed did not believe the fishing stocks would last to provide the next generation with a living. Rather than condemn their children to a gruelling job

which leads to physical exhaustion at 40, they dreamt of giving them an education.

'My dream is to make enough money to send my children to high school so they can get a job in a grocery store,' explained a 39-year-old mother of 11. She also prays, because she knows God hears her prayers.

Philrads has helped these families in several ways. Firstly, they have provided a bigger boat which allows the fishermen to combine their efforts for a bigger catch. In turn a church has grown up directly as a result of the fishing project. Philrads has provided a village clinic for vaccination and health education.

Thinking ahead saves lives
Thanks to a special emergency relief fund provided in advance by Tear Fund, its Philippine partner, Philrads, was able to act swiftly when an earthquake hit the northern Philippines in July 1990. With 1,500 people dead and as many as 790,000 homeless, there was no time for committee meetings or even telegrams to England. Instead, Philrads reacted immediately by providing food, tents, blankets and medical supplies for 2,600 families.

Relief . . . then rehabilitation
They sent five relief teams into the worst affected areas in the north of the main island of Luzon. This included the city of Banguio which suffered the heaviest casualties and worst damage, and which was virtually isolated when landslides blocked roads and cut off supplies. Devastation was so severe that one town, the City of Pines, was renamed City of the Dead when funeral parlours could no longer accommodate the earthquake's victims.

The Philippines, a submerged chain of mountains which form more than 7,000 islands, is prone to disasters: seasonal typhoons, flooding, landslides, drought, volcanic eruption and earthquakes. Each year Filipinos experience approximately 20 typhoons, and each time they can look to Philrads for swift action. Church buildings become shelters, the congregations a committed team of volunteers. Philrads are soon on the scene – often the first agency to arrive. They bring resources, expertise and organisation to the chaos.

Naturally, Tear Fund's help does not end after each disaster; Philrads' rehabilitation work continues long afterwards: development always follows disaster.

Garth Hewitt – a voice for the voiceless
Garth's first memory of Tear Fund is doing a presentation in 1973 at George Hoffman's request. He then narrated the filmstrip *Walk in*

Partner Portrait

Jun Vencer of Philrads: 'Poor is no Excuse'

Growing up among poverty and malnutrition in the barrios (slum areas), then fighting his way through city life, Jun saw the struggles of the disadvantaged first-hand. Beginning as a medical student but finally qualifying as a lawyer, he questioned the Christian faith until convinced intellectually. But after committing his life to Christ, his probing and challenging were not over.

There is a co-operative tradition in the barrio when all the men and women of the neighbourhood work together. But where do you see evangelicals co-operating with one another?' The gospel can't be communicated unless you do it in the context of poverty and justice. If only we could work together to show the love of Christ in practical, ambitious ways to the rest of Philippine society, I'm convinced that our unity would be a lot stronger.

This was the challenge facing Jun and the Philippine Council of Evangelical Churches (PCEC). As a result of his concern, the Philippines Relief and Development Services, Philrads, grew up. In some ways it is the Philippines' equivalent of Tear Fund because it grew out of PCEC in the same way that Tear Fund grew out of the Evangelical Alliance.

Since Tear Fund first worked with Philrads it has made grants totalling almost £1 million. In 1992 Jun became the first International Director of World Evangelical Fellowship from the developing world. His achievements and those of Philrads owe much to the advice of his grandfather, a wise man from Nueva Sevilla, the *Broken Image* fishing community: 'Poor is no excuse for not doing your best.'

His Shoes. He also wrote various audio-visual scripts and a number of songs, among which was *A World of Difference.*

In 1978 Garth visited the Third World for the first time – Haiti and the Dominican Republic – with the aim of writing songs for the impending International Year of the Child. The theme tune for the filmstrip *Tomorrow's World,* sung by a Haitian blind school, came from a simple chant sung by field workers.

The influence of the Haiti trip was to take over much of what Garth did and was influential in his forming the Amos Trust in 1985 to cover the expenses of his increasing involvement in the Third World.

On a tour to India with Stephen Rand, Garth met Mother Teresa of Calcutta and wrote the songs *Road to Freedom* (which became the title of his first UK tour for Tear Fund) and *Water, water.*

'Christianity made visible' sums up Tear Fund for Garth, and he was particularly keen to help convey a message of justice for the poor to the British Christian public. In 1982 he said, 'The content of most British gospel music is pretty thin. The message is basically "Come to Jesus." I want people to listen to the lyrics of these songs and take them seriously.'

Mindo Rondael from Philrads in conversation with Stewart Henderson, Geoffrey Stephenson and Garth Hewitt during their visit.

CHAPTER NINE

INDIA: A HEART FOR THE POOR

'God wanted me in the slums'

This is the claim of a remarkable Indian woman doctor, who turned her back on a lucrative career as a doctor to Delhi's middle classes at the age of 26. When a cholera epidemic struck Delhi in the summer of 1988, Dr Kiran Martin began a small health clinic with a borrowed table and chair.

She turned for support to one of Tear Fund's partners, the Emmanuel Hospital Association, and saw the beginning of the project called ASHA – the Hindi word for hope – and the acronym for Action for Securing Health for All.

Under Kiran Martin's enthusiastic and dynamic leadership, the ASHA team expanded, taking on a number of doctors and nurses, many of whom were Christians.

Together they provide basic healthcare for slum families, India's outcasts, who cannot afford private treatment and who are generally mistrustful of the overburdened government health service.

After a few months the project was visited by officials from the Delhi Development Authority. 'They were shocked to find a group of professional doctors working in those conditions,' says Kiran Martin. But that visit was the start of a supportive relationship, particularly with Slum Commissioner Mr Manjit Singh, a senior Delhi civil servant who had grown up in the slums. He encouraged ASHA to expand its vital work into 15 slums, providing healthcare for one-tenth of Delhi's slum people.

As a result of this pioneering relationship, the government has dug deep-bore water pumps, installed toilet blocks and drainage, and built health clinics, all in response to requests from the slum-dwellers themselves, helped by Dr Martin's team who act as mediators to bridge the gap between the government and slum-dwellers. ASHA's commitment has been to staff the health centres and pay for running costs, supported by Tear Fund.

In two years ASHA had trained 80 community health workers, mainly women in distinctive sky blue saris, each of whom is responsible for 300 families.

Former *Tear Times* editor John Capon, who visited the ASHA project, was unrestrained in his praise of Dr Martin. 'She had so much get up and go, and dealt with the government officials so successfully – I saw her as the next Mother Teresa.'

The jewel in Tear Fund's crown?
Over the past 25 years, Tear Fund has, appropriately, given more money to India than any other single nation, working with a total of 38 Indian partners.

One of Tear Fund's other 'special relationships' is with its Indian partner EFICOR, the Evangelical Fellowship of India Commission on Relief. EFICOR received its first Tear Fund grant in September 1972, and by the early 1990s had made good use of over £2 million, specialising in helping local churches in disaster emergencies, well-drilling, agriculture, training and community development throughout India.

For C. B. Samuel, Director of EFICOR, the right sort of partnership is crucial. 'We need to take Jesus' understanding of the nature of money as a spiritual force (Mammon) seriously.

Any relationship that is based on dealing with money is not merely a financial transaction but a spiritual transaction. It is sad but true that if the money factor was withdrawn, many partnerships would simply end.'

With Tear Fund he shares a concern to move into what he calls 'the third level of partnership', beyond purely funding and resources, a relationship where he says, 'we relate not by our ability to give or receive but as partners in suffering and pain, in joy and celebration. Our professionalism must be clothed with the compassion of God.'

Breaking through the silence

Another word for 'hope', this time in Tamil, is *Nambikkai*, the title of a Tear Fund video about another pioneering work, this time on the southernmost tip of India. Ian Stillman, an Englishman, and himself profoundly deaf, went to India in 1975 to set up a project for the hard of hearing in India.

With Tear Fund's assistance, he bought a 42-acre plot with agricultural potential, which is now a caring community offering general education, vocational training, farming, an employment scheme for girls, residential programmes and camps or retreats for the deaf.

Deaf people are at the bottom of the agenda in India, a land still largely ruled by caste structure and superstition. Deafness is seen as a curse from God, whereas in reality rubella accounts for some 29 per cent of cases, around 24 per cent of cases may be the result of close inter-marriages, and 40 per cent of all cases are preventable.

Deaf women in particular are seen as unmarriageable, so a major part of the work of Ian's Indian wife Sue is to help arrange marriages!

Partner Portrait

Vijayan and Premila Pavamani
Emmanuel Ministries

In early 1971, Vijayan Pavamani, Director of Youth for Christ in India, and his wife Premila, opened their home in the compound of St Paul's Cathedral, Calcutta, to people in distress. Out of that grew the Calcutta Samaritans, with which Vijayan is still involved today.

Many of the people they helped in those days were addicts, which led to Vijayan founding his own base for drug addicts in 1977. Beginning with a small hired room in the centre of Calcutta, they offered counselling and residential rehabilitation. 'We have seen Christ do for individuals what years of treatment, medicine and hospitalisation could not do,' Vijayan commented in 1978.

A year later, with assistance from Tear Fund, to ensure less temptation for their recovering addicts, they bought a property outside Calcutta which they named the Midway Home. Moved by the plight of local 'railway children', fending for themselves on Howrah station after being abandoned, he and Premila started to take some of them into their home, eventually setting up a separate home for them which provided food, clothing, schooling and medical treatment. There was also work with prostitutes and the men from West Bengal who stream into Calcutta at the rate of about 1,000 a day and usually end up as rickshaw pullers. The Pavamanis helped these people manage their affairs, providing shelter so they could send money home to their families.

All this work eventually came under the umbrella of Emmanuel Ministries, one of Tear Fund's 38 partners in India.

'Vijayan is a visionary,' explains Jennie Evans, who has known the Pavamanis for many years. 'He has a tremendous heart for people, for children, men and women. Tear Fund has had to work out how to pace its support, ensuring that he is taking on something manageable!'

The Pavamanis ran the risk of dissipating all their resources in response to the immediate needs of those around them. The danger of exhaustion leading to breakdown, burn-out or paralysis was ever present. The Pavamani family was given more adequate facilities to enable them to continue in sacrificial service beyond the depletion of their own basic means.

For Tear Fund's Tenth Anniversary Meetings in February 1979, Vijayan and Premila Pavamani visited various parts of Britain to contribute to its 'Stop, step back and think' programmes. Despite being stranded by snow in Newcastle, Vijayan's message, based on the Bible story of the man who saw clearly after a second touch from Jesus, was heard by thousands of supporters as Tear Fund fulfilled its aim of encouraging Third World partners to speak for themselves.

Water

Water is certainly on Tear Fund's priority list – helping people obtain a clean, regular and free supply of water can break the poverty chain. For years it has recognised that water is their most basic physical need and a vital resource; yet water is also the greatest cause of disease in the Two Thirds World.

Seven out of ten people who live in country areas of the Third World are without clean water.

80 per cent of all disease in the world today is caused by polluted water.

40,000 people die every day because of preventable disease caused by malnutrition and inadequate water supplies.

A bigger splash

Water engineer Roger Holland from Coulsdon, Surrey, went to Burundi, Africa, with an extraordinary pedigree. During the 1980s he helped construct the Grand Canyon Rapids Ride at Alton Towers Theme Park in Staffordshire! Having been instrumental in giving millions of visitors to Alton Towers the thrill of their lives, he next committed himself to the Buhiga Mission, supervising the installation of clean water supplies for remote village communities. At least no one poured cold water on his plans . . .

India:
a heart for the poor

Disappearing food

Traditional taboos are to blame for a great deal of food losses through pests. The Hindu veneration of animals, for example, which hinders adequate pest and vermin control, results in huge food losses in India. In Uttar Pradesh, it is said, rats alone consume no less than ten million tons of grain a year. It is estimated that in the whole of India rats eat enough food each year to support 100 million people. According to one survey, nearly one-third of all the food grown in poor countries is lost through disease, insects and other pests, either before or after harvest. Even when sufficient food has been produced following a good harvest, the farmers have difficulty in storing any surpluses and bringing them to market.

Western greed

Some of the blame for malnutrition in developing countries can be attributed directly to the West. People in poor countries eat almost all of their grain directly. In rich countries, grain is eaten indirectly via meat. Since we eat so much meat, one-third of the world's cereal production goes to fatten beef cattle and other livestock, which is a very inefficient way of using grain. According to a US Department of Agriculture report, it takes seven pounds of grain to produce one pound of edible beef.

Not surprisingly, grain consumption per person in the West is more than two and a half times that of the Third World. A distressing side-effect of this imbalance is that Africa has been a net exporter of protein to Europe at a time when many of its people across the continent faced starvation.

Tear Fund Tea – refreshing news!

Launched in 1982 at 78p for 250g, Tear Fund Tea was tea with a difference. 'We needed to take note of the X Factor – Christian involvement,' announced *Tear Times*.

Tear Fund Tea was pure Assam from the Mornai estate, possibly the only tea estate in the world run by a Christian organisation. Unlike many supermarket blends, it is not mixed with leaves from other estates. Instead it is properly picked at peak growing times, processed, graded, quality-controlled, packed and sealed in India, before despatch as a speciality tea for a discerning public.

CHAPTER TEN

UGANDA: COMPASSION HAS THE HEART

Cliff finds concern, not condemnation

An extraordinary mixture of joys and sorrows confronted Cliff Richard when he visited Uganda in 1992 to make a video, *Compassion has the Heart*.

As well as showing how the Church in Uganda is responding positively to the AIDS crisis, bringing a message of hope to counteract the growing fatalism in the country, the team found other encouraging results of Tear Fund's support. In south-west Uganda, they saw how Kagando hospital had grown into a centre of hope and health for thousands of people.

Opened in 1965, the hospital is now part of the Kagando Rural Development Centre, a total community development project in a poor area where the first secondary school only opened in 1979.

That was also the year that British doctors, nurses, midwives, builders and agriculturists were first sent by Tear Fund to Kagando to assist the work of missionaries and Ugandan staff. Since then Tear Fund has given grants for buildings, vehicles for its community health programme, a tractor hire scheme, purchase of cows and an oil press for the agricultural side of the work, as well as drugs and equipment for Kagando Hospital itself.

Of all the projects, the major one was a £200,000 hydro-electric scheme completed in 1987, towards which Tear Fund gave £40,000. The hydro-turbine generator powered by water from a nearby river ensured the operating theatre, intensive care unit and delivery suite had proper lighting and power at all times. Before then, operations had been performed in dim light to the accompaniment of a noisy generator and sometimes torchlight had to suffice. Sterilisation of instruments depended on an inefficient charcoal-heated pressure cooker!

The arrival of electricity at Kagando Hospital was an occasion for great rejoicing in the community. The Ugandan Ministers for Health and Co-operatives performed the opening ceremony for the hydro-electric plant and a new out-patients department. Juliet Brown, a former Tear Fund member of staff at the hospital, said, 'Kagando Hospital has become a "light on a hill" in more ways than one. God has provided light for the hospital, for which we thank him. Please

continue to pray for the staff at Kagando, that they will be a light to those they meet and serve.'

One hospital – thousands of lives

With mothers sleeping below their children's beds and relatives cooking patients' food, conditions at Kagando seem basic compared to British hospitals. Yet Kagando has had a major impact on people's health in south-west Uganda. Dr Paul Saunderson, who worked at Kagando Hospital from 1981–87 and was Medical Superintendent for two years, estimates that Kagando performs around 80 per cent of the work of a Western hospital at about 1 per cent of the cost. By the time he left Kagando there were 120 hospital staff and four doctors.

'Before 1965 there was no health care in the area to speak of. Many women were dying in labour and malnutrition was widespread, particularly kwashiorkor which is caused by lack of protein.'

Throughout the 1970s Kagando concentrated on maternal and child health and started to train local health workers in clinics around the country.

The end of President Amin's notorious rule in 1979 saw an upturn in the nation's prosperity and health and Kagando benefited accordingly.

In 1979 Paul Saunderson's predecessor, Dr Rob Morris, initiated a community-based vaccination programme against polio, diphtheria, whooping cough, measles and tetanus which has probably saved thousands of lives. 'You used to see cases of neo-natal tetanus regularly, simply because the mothers were not immunised,' says Paul Saunderson.

Other improvements have been in simple dentistry and eye care. Under ophthalmologist Dr Keith Waddell (the hospital's medical superintendent from 1965–79), the eye unit treated eye diseases and made glasses for the many people over 50 who otherwise could not read.

Kampala Baptist Church wanted to help the children orphaned by AIDS. They started the Kampala Baptist Student Project and with the help of Tear Fund and Compassion International, the project now pays for about 375 children to go to local schools. The project also provides food, clothes and health care for the children. Some of the children who join the scheme have never been to school before, so the church has a special 'catch up' school which they attend until ready for normal school. And on Saturdays, they learn skills which will help them earn a living later on.

One special grant of £3,500 from Tear Fund supported a schools drama programme that combined health education with a presentation of the gospel.

Today, however, at least half the hospital's admissions are AIDS-related. During his own time at Kagando, Paul Saunderson saw the numbers of cases increase from occasional incidents in 1985 to one a day by 1987. Now there is a very active programme of counselling and home visits for those with AIDS.

Meanwhile Paul became deeply involved in another area of health care, which to him is as vital as AIDS work. Having gained a Diploma in Tropical Medicine in 1984, he left Kagando in 1987 to devote himself to leprosy and TB control, co-ordinating the work of a Leprosy Control project in the South and West Provinces. Leprosy and tuberculosis are caused by similar bacteria and need a year for treatment, the only two diseases to require such lengthy care.

Five years later Paul is optimistic that leprosy will soon be eradicated in Uganda. 'We have very effective drug treatment and it does not seem to be affected by the spread of AIDS.'

Sufferers from TB, on the other hand, are victims of the 'Cinderella' of the medical world. Although almost non-existent in the West, an estimated 8–9 million people contract TB each year, of whom three million die. And TB is one of the most common diseases to attack an AIDS sufferer, eventually proving fatal. 'Work in TB is more a holding operation than something that is likely to lead to eradication,' Paul told Tear Fund's Uganda supporters in 1991. Yet there were encouragements, through immunisation and drug programmes, and Paul was able to work with Ugandan doctors who would in turn become responsible for the control programmes.

Paul is in no doubt that leprosy and TB control was as vital as AIDS work, because he has been able to see results during his term of service: 'I often wonder if I've been responsible for saving more lives through the TB programme than through running a hospital!'

AIDS – the silent holocaust

AIDS is decimating Africa, no more so than Uganda.

Already in some areas, one in ten children are orphans. There are an estimated 600,000 to 1.2 million orphans in Uganda; many are victims of HIV. One in eight Ugandan adults is already infected

with HIV, mostly among the 20–35-year-olds. Thousands of babies are born HIV positive, many of them die before they are two. Others are left as orphans. Often weak, old grandparents have to look after 15 or 16 children, because their sons and daughters have died. They don't have enough money to buy them food, clothes or medicine, let alone pay school fees.

The Church gives practical and medical help to people with AIDS. There are mission hospitals like Mengo, and Community Centres

have been opened where people can be tested, receive treatment and talk to trained counsellors about the problems they face.

Bulange Community Centre was opened in April 1990. Each Wednesday a doctor comes to the clinic and people with AIDS can come for treatment. As one of the main problems for AIDS sufferers is loneliness caused by prejudice, it is encouraging to see helpers and people with AIDS worshipping together, despite all their problems.

Experts predict that more people could die of AIDS during the next ten years than from all the wars and natural disasters of the last 50.

The Church is in a unique and challenging position as AIDS devastates many developing countries. Tear Fund is supporting and encouraging the Church as it responds with compassion for those who suffer, as well as with health education programmes and a biblical message of one faithful partner for life. 'Behaviour change' is regarded as a key message in AIDS education. Christians in Uganda believe that Jesus can bring lasting 'behaviour change'.

Partner Portrait

Bishop Misaeri Kauma of Namirembe Diocese, Church of Uganda

Talking with Bishop Misaeri Kauma about the Church's Health Programme, Cliff found concern, not condemnation, for people with AIDS.

Bishop Misaeri Kauma loves his country and longs to see the current political stability consolidated after 20 years of civil war. Meanwhile he has received encouragement from the head of state, President Museveni, in tackling the problem of AIDS in Uganda. 'His Excellency was one of the very first men to come out and say, "In Uganda there's AIDS. Don't hide it." This helped us because everybody in Uganda now knows there is the danger of AIDS,' the Bishop explains.

As one of the first within the Church to recognise and tackle the problem of AIDS in his country, Bishop Misaeri Kauma has made special efforts to reach his people, especially the youth, with the biblical answer to AIDS. Communication is poor in Uganda, so in 1989 Tear Fund helped him circulate a letter to the one million homes and 700 congregations in Namirembe Diocese, which covers much of Kampala, Uganda's capital, and includes some of the most densely populated slums in the country. Printed in the local language of Luganda, it gave correct medical information on AIDS written from a biblical viewpoint.

'The Church is the right place to tell people about sexuality,' he said at the time. 'We teach the proper limits for sex. It is a great moral opportunity.'

His diocese also set up a pastoral care programme for AIDS sufferers, to help patients, their families, and now, sadly, the increasing number of orphans left destitute by the disease. When one parent has died from AIDS, it is almost certain that the other will die too. The Bishop has had 'hundreds of people' arrive at his office, desperate to know who will care for their deceased relatives' children.

They say, 'Mother died last year. Father has just died. They are left behind and what to do? I've got 12 of my own. I can't take them over. Bishop or the Church, can you help? They need fees. They need clothing, medical care. They need somewhere to sleep. Bishop, can you tell our friends to help us?'

As a nation we are challenged to find a solution. We are very glad because Tear Fund in England has helped our diocese and many other areas to care for orphaned children. Also to care for the sick and help give education to the population about AIDS.

Realising that the hospitals would soon be too full to care for people with AIDS, Bishop Misaeri's diocesan health programme started training 'Good Samaritan' teams of church members to care for

Beatrice (in pink) is counselling an AIDS patient at Mengo Hospital, Uganda, with Rev Agatha Senyimba looking on. After Beatrice's husband died as a result of AIDS, she was comforted by another widow: 'I coped because I saw someone caring for me who had the same problem. I decided I would help others, too, and share my experiences with them.'

people with AIDS in their homes. They go out to feed them, pray with them, read the Bible with them and, especially, bring them to faith before they die.

Bishop Misaeri is utterly confident that he and his workers are following in Jesus' footsteps. 'The Church here is involved because we know God loves people. The Church is here for the sinful like a hospital is for the sick. You don't get healthy people in hospital. We feel it is our responsibility to be with those who are suffering.'

Convinced since the age of 19 that Jesus is his personal Saviour, Bishop Misaeri delights in sharing his faith. He is especially touched that the Church's help has reduced the number of suicides amongst those with AIDS. 'When they come to know Jesus, we find their suffering is eased because they know they have got a Saviour who cares.'

The Bishop has hope for his country's future.

As Jesus is alive, we should be full hope. I am sure AIDS won't be here forever. I haven't heard of any nation that has found a solution to AIDS. So we have turned to prayer. God said, 'When you pray, I will answer.' And God is answering. So I take that in faith and I believe AIDS will be a foundation stone for a great future because God is teaching us great lessons through it.

The AIDS prayer

Almighty God, heavenly Father, who enabled your servant Job to go victoriously through great bodily suffering without denying your name, power and love, have mercy on us, Lord, who are stricken by this epidemic of AIDS. Stretch out your healing hand and hold back this virus. Strengthen and comfort in Jesus Christ those infected and ease their pain of body and mind. Send your Holy Spirit to renew us all and lead us into repentance and faith in the gospel.

Give us the gift of discipline that we may keep our bodies and minds clean and holy. Grant wisdom, knowledge and perseverance to all who are sick and are seeking that they might find the drugs to prevent and heal the disease. Have mercy on us, Lord, and on all AIDS sufferers throughout the world. Give love and compassion to all those sick to help them. Through Jesus Christ our Lord. Amen.

(Bishop Misaeri Kauma)

Tear Fund's response to AIDS

Tear Fund allocated more than £400,000 to AIDS projects in 1992 alone and is seeking to encourage and equip its partners around the world to develop a Christian response to the global AIDS epidemic. Here are some of the projects they are supporting:

- **Education and prevention**
  'The Family, God's Answer to AIDS': Tear Fund has given £4,000 to a key Scripture Union education project in Zimbabwe of this name, one of many around the world.
- **Orphan care**
  Tear Fund has given £30,000 to the evangelistic organisation, Uganda Women Concern Ministry, to support its project in Mbale which provides orphans with healthcare, counselling and school fees.
- **Home care**
  The millions with AIDS cannot be cared for in hospitals. In Chiang Mai, Thailand, a grant of £46,000 enabled ACT, AIDS Counselling and Training, to expand their counselling work so their workers could receive training in home care, as well as a vehicle to reach their patients.
- **Medical care**
  With £46,000 from Tear Fund, Intermission, a Christian agency working in a Bombay Muslim slum, started a health clinic focussing on AIDS.
- **Counselling**
  Tear Fund allocated £2,000 for a series of short courses training church leaders in AIDS counselling at Kenya's Daystar Bible College, one of many key partners encouraging sensitive, professional and spiritually strong counselling.

Programmes of hope

Along with its partners, Tear Fund believes that community involvement is the only way to bring about lasting change in the AIDS crisis. Changing behaviour is more than either simply a moral issue (faithfulness) or practical issue (using condoms). Dr Ian Campbell of the Salvation Army believes that whole countries like Uganda can change their behaviour: 'The depth of work and understanding needed to change behaviour are remarkable. Tear Fund is facilitating programmes of hope all over the world, because they are well put together, community-based and bathed in a strong sense of faith.' In 1993 Rev David Evans joined Tear Fund's staff team as its HIV–Aids consultant.

CHAPTER ELEVEN

BRAZIL: CHILDREN ON THE EDGE

'Our greatest needs are often stated in terms of our children. So are our greatest hopes. When poverty affects adults, it strikes children all the more. Adults grow ill. Children die. Adults get hungry. Children starve.'

So writes Dr Wess Stafford, President of Compassion International, Tear Fund's partner organisation in child development. Tear Fund's *Partners in Childcare* scheme has been limked to the US based Compassion International since 1974.

Every day, 40,000 children aged 15 and under die from poverty-related causes. Comparing this figure to the air disaster at Lockerbie on 21st December 1988, which killed 270 people, Dr Stafford estimated that it would take a Lockerbie tragedy every ten minutes to match the daily horror of children's deaths.

Children are the most vulnerable group in society but also have enormous potential. Child development is a special focus of Tear Fund's ministry. Over 24,000 individual children are supported

through the *Partners in Childcare* programme, provided with food, clothing, healthcare and a Christian education.

Streets leading nowhere

100 million street children roam the world's cities

About 100 million children survive by prostitution, theft and begging, eking out a threadbare existence as modern-day 'David Copperfields' in a world that has all but forgotten them.

This was the finding of a six-day conference on street children, held in May 1989 in the Philippines, home to the largest number of street children in South-east Asia. Funded by the private charity Childhope and the United Nations Children's Fund, the First Regional Conference on Street Children in Asia ended with a pledge by the 24 participating Asian and Pacific nations to raise public and private funds to finance a three-year relief project for street children and enact laws to protect them.

Sadly the problem did not vanish in three years. The problem remains because the underlying conditions remain. Most street children have been abandoned by parents who flocked to crowded cities from impoverished rural areas of the Third World but found they lacked the skills to find decent jobs.

Parents often sell children, both boys and girls, to prostitution and crime syndicates because they are desperate for money.

'The kids are being exchanged for refrigerators and television sets,' reported Peter Tacon of Childhope during the conference.

Shamingly, it is often citizens from Western nations who exploit these children as they beg motorists for coins in traffic jams, peddle cigarettes, newspapers and flowers and offer themselves to foreign tourists for money or a decent meal.

This was the case in Sao Paulo, Brazil's largest city, which Ulster TV journalist Paul Clark visited with a Tear Fund video team in 1991. From a hillside outside the city, the pale, majestic skyscrapers gave an impression of prosperity. But Sao Paulo has been called a concrete jungle and down on the streets the reality of another maxim could be seen, namely that in Sao Paulo 'You are either rich, poor or very poor.'

Ten per cent of the citizens live in *favelas*, or shanty towns. Beneath a flyover Paul met a young pastor who had given up a secure bank job to shepherd a particularly disadvantaged flock; this favella was situated next to a rubbish tip between two railway lines. 'These are people whom most would prefer to ignore or forget,' said Paul. A few yards away from piles of rubbish and the broken furniture which provided homes for the pastor's congregation, he opened two sheet doors to reveal a small, whitewashed chapel where he held his services.

Sao Paulo's mirage of prosperity attracts impoverished people from the countryside; surely they will find work in the world's second largest city? They soon find, however, that the streets are not paved with gold and at this point, with no welfare state to rescue them, they are frequently forced to abandon their children because they cannot provide for them.

'The children become the ultimate victims of poverty,' Paul reported. 'Around one million beg for food and steal on the streets of Sao Paulo.'

The children face an even greater danger than malnourishment. Some of the more prosperous citizens and even some of the police have decided that the way to deal with the problem of unwanted children is to shoot them; the discoveries of young, bound bodies have horrified those who have read about them, including the Brazilians. Many individuals are trying to do something to alleviate this situation. There are also church-based initiatives, and Tear Fund has been closely involved with Jonathan Santos, whose Antioch Mission has a special programme to help give a few of the wild, unwanted street children a normal childhood.

Good news on the streets
Looking at Marcilio Jesosa with the boys in his care today, it is hard to imagine him as a seven-year-old high on drugs. But at that age he had already left home, as a result of his parents drinking and

beating him. After six years in prison for stealing to pay for his drugs, he went back to the streets until further trouble with the police drove him to the Church for help. 'My life completely changed. I met Jesus and God put his love in my heart. I wanted to share this good news with the children on the street.'

Today Marcilio is a reformed drug addict working for the Antioch Mission, an organisation which seeks to take the gospel out into the world while remembering its own children at home. Marcilio runs one of two Rescue Centres for street children in Sao Paulo. He is a father figure to 22 boys aged between eight and fourteen, with the job of giving them shelter, food and some basic education, as well as an opportunity to hear about Jesus Christ.

Partner Portrait

Jonathan Santos, Antioch Mission, Brazil

In 1961, pastor Jonathan Santos started a small Bible School for local people in a small village deep in the interior of Brazil. Jonathan's vision was to prepare Christians for mission, and soon other churches grew from his school.

Next his family moved to Sao Paulo, which saw the development of the Antioch Mission, a thriving indigenous mission agency with 45 people serving in 13 countries, including China, Africa and the UK.

'But we can't forget the needs on our doorstep,' says Jonathan. The Mission's headquarters consists of several ministries, with a Bible School and children's home centring on a Prayer Centre. It is here, to the 'Valley of Blessing', that street children are brought to be gently restored to the sort of family life that British children take for granted. They recover from street life in small family units, while the Mission finds families to foster or adopt them.

'We receive them into our programme and help them get reintegrated,' explains Jonathan. 'They have to be healed spiritually and emotionally – in soul and spirit – and then we look for a home for them.'

Good News to the Poor shows the children who may never have used a pencil learning to write and draw, sitting at little tables, like a normal primary school. One little boy is seen standing on tiptoe in his pyjamas by the stove, watching the woman cooking his supper. This domesticity is all part of the reintegration programme, a major change for children who have scrounged for food.

Journalist Paul Clark arrived on a day when a farewell party for a little boy was taking place; he had been adopted, and although he would never know the precise date of his birthday, there was every likelihood that he would have a more secure and happy future.

Restoring 22 boys at a time out of the seven million estimated to be on the streets of Brazil is only a drop of hope in an ocean of neglect. Jonathan wishes he could help more, explaining that they are doing all they can at the moment. What is the next step? 'We have to pray and wait on the Lord.'

But the work has been started and the opportunity for committed people to help is there.

Since 1985 Tear Fund has allocated £40,000 towards building costs and resources for the Bible School and children's accommodation. Local churches help with clothing, food and voluntary help for the street children, but Jonathan nonetheless believes more Brazilian Christians must be challenged to help.

'We believe the gospel is good news,' says Jonathan. 'We have seen it transform lives, all around the world, and right here on the streets of Sao Paulo.'

One opportunity for a positive involvement with under-privileged children is through Tear Fund's *Partners in Childcare* scheme. Just £13 a month spells the difference between education and lack of skills, food and hunger, shoes and bare feet.

The scheme provides school fees and basic medical care. It is usually administered through a local church in the region. It is the church that recommends needy families and oversees the process in co-operation with the family. Support for a child frequently benefits the rest of the family because often a child will come home from school and share what he has learnt with them. This has resulted in mothers, as well as brothers and sisters, learning to read and write. Similarly, since a condition of the scheme is to provide a Christian education, some parents have become Christians through their supported child's contact with the local church.

The scheme provides a delightful point of contact between different cultures. Childcare supporters may be old or young, single or married, and come from all over Britain and Ireland. If they have children of their own, the link gives them an awareness of the Third World while they are young.

Although dealing with over 24,000 supporters, Child Development Manager Carole Allen and her colleagues try to be available to help with queries. 'We hope supporters will feel able to approach us with their problems and queries,' she says.

The growth in popularity of the *Partners in Childcare* scheme has benefited thousands of children in poorer countries and has laid a foundation for their futures where there was otherwise little hope.

Going to school

In the rich world, nine out of ten children have secondary education, compared to four out of ten in the poor world.

Nearly half the funds allocated in Tear Fund's *Childcare* programme go to school projects, enabling children from poor families

to attend church-run schools in areas where there are few if any
government schools. Children unable to study in their homes, which
might be cramped, crowded shacks, can go to an increasing number
of student centres, where they receive extra help and tuition on top
of what they learn at school.

In many of the programmes, education carries on after classes finish, as the children are taught how to plant trees, how to live safely
with water, practising elementary sanitation and hygiene, how to
play in teams and take responsibility. Needless to say, they have a
lot to share with their brothers and sisters when they get home.

Training for life

Every child receives Christian training through Sunday School or
Bible class, to encourage them to learn about Jesus Christ and to
grow and develop in their faith. Tear Fund believes that this concern
for the whole person is a vital part of child development.

These are the immediate benefits. Other benefits will be felt many
years later, when the young adult is more likely to get a good job
which will benefit his or her family and the community.

This is where Tear Fund's *Partners in Training* scheme comes in.
It provides the funds which enable many thousands of young people
to receive two or more years' training in skills which will give them
a profession and a future. At rural youth polytechnics, hospitals,
city industrial colleges and mechanical workshops on almost every
continent, enthusiastic young men and women are receiving training, thanks to Tear Fund supporters. Incredibly, this only requires
a minimum donation of £10 a month. Many young people, such as
nurses and doctors, are so appreciative of the help and training they
have received that they choose to remain in their communities in
order to serve their own people.

Equally vital, *Partners in Training* directly helps the fast-growing
Church in the Third World by training several hundred national
pastors and lay leaders. Bearing in mind that the Church is often the
most consistent institution in some politically unstable countries,
this aspect of the scheme makes a significant contribution to the
spiritual health of these nations.

> Four out of five children in the Third World have never seen
> a health worker. One in ten children in the Third World dies
> before its first birthday.

No fault of their own

The distended stomachs of starving Third World children so often
seen on Western TV screens can have a more complex origin than
just lack of food. It may be due to kwashiorkor, which is caused

by lack of protein and is found in many parts of South-east Asia and throughout Africa. Children become apathetic, their stomachs distend, their muscles waste away and their skin discolours before they succumb to the full effects of the disease.

Another disease to which children are prey is marasmus, with similar symptoms, caused by starvation. An Indian government report in the 1980s revealed that four million of the 23 million babies born there each year will die before reaching the age of four.

Death: the tip of the iceberg

That same Indian government report also revealed that 16 million of the children who survived beyond their fourth birthday would suffer some form of physical or mental handicap because of under-nourishment.

So often disease can be prevented by the sort of vitamin-rich diet which the British government both helps provide through benefits and educates its mothers to expect. Here are some examples.

Vitamin A deficiency	A major cause of blindness in Asia and Latin America
Vitamin B deficiency	Occurs mainly in Asian countries; causes beri-beri, a wasting and paralysis of the limbs
Vitamin D deficiency	Causes rickets, leading to deformities of the skull, legs, spine and pelvis
Iron deficiency	Causes anaemias which result in general ill-health and inactivity

In addition to these specific diseases, children's resistance to infection is greatly lowered by malnutrition.

Many of the causes of malnutrition are deeply ingrained in traditional culture or relate to external factors. A major problem of the Third World is its debt to Western banks. Each year many countries give half or even all their total export earnings in debt repayments. For instance, shortly before the famine in 1986, Sudan had increased its food exports threefold in an effort to gain foreign exchange and relieve its debt burden.

The African famine which inspired so many in the Western world to give, and which also compelled governments to give aid, brought in some three and a half billion dollars to be spent on African relief in 1985. What is not so widely known is that also in 1985 the 29 poorest countries in Africa paid back to the industrialised countries *twice* this amount in interest payments on their debts. Early in 1987, Brazil announced that for the foreseeable future it did not intend to repay either the interest or the capital on £60 billion of commercial bank loans. It is just one of the countries where the international debt crisis hurts the poorest people the most.

Such situations illustrate the need to 'teach people how to fish' as well as just giving them their daily bread. This is where Tear Fund comes in, with the ideas and resources for small-scale self-help; thousands of projects worldwide have been undertaken over the past 25 years. Directly and indirectly, these projects have improved the health of the world's children.

Each year the harvest is big enough to feed one and a half times the world's population ... Yet 100 million children go to bed hungry each night – that's almost twice the population of the United Kingdom.

'Why do they have so many children?'

This is a common response from exasperated Westerners. But for many families in developing countries, children are their only security for the future. In the absence of a welfare state providing old age pensions and health care, it is seen as only sensible to ensure you have at least two sons to support you in your old age. Thus poverty is the cause of large families, rather than the other way round. When Cliff Richard visited a child being helped through Tear Fund in Haiti, his father introduced him as 'my walking stick for my old age'.

Sally Lambert began Tear Fund's ministry to children in 1974, having served with the South American Missionary Society. When she joined Tear Fund, there was a staff of around 15 and an annual income of less than £1 million.

A former nurse and secretary, Sally was the natural choice to handle the launch of Tear Fund's child development scheme in conjunction with Compassion International. Beginning with a few hundred children, she saw the scheme grow to around 18,000, a figure which is constantly increasing. Over the years she visited many of the children Tear Fund sponsored in Asia, Africa and Latin America. Her open, friendly nature and obvious affection for the children endeared her to Tear Fund's overseas partners.

After 15 years, Sally laid down her role as Director of the Overseas Family Care Department. In that time, tens of thousands of Third World children, young people and families had benefited from Sally's work and extensive travels.

Children's rights
In 1989 the United Nations General Assembly adopted the Convention on the Rights of the Child, understood to be any person under 18, and which says:

Every child has the right to life, nationality, freedom of speech and belief.

In reality:

100,000 illegal abortions are performed each day of the year

The Convention says:

Every child has the right to education, and development in all areas of the child's personality and talents

In reality:

In 1990 approximately 100 million six to eleven-year-olds did not attend school; 60 per cent of them were girls

The convention says:

Every child has the right to health, food and clean water

In reality:

In the 1990s, it is estimated that 130 million children will die of disease and malnutrition

The Convention says:

A child has the right to protection from exploitation, physical and sexual abuse, and abandonment

In reality:

It is estimated that 80 million children are exploited as child workers. An estimated 200,000 under-fifteens have been recruited into military forces in recent years, forced to kill and die.

> . . . our whole perception of the concept of a 'disaster' has much more to do with social and political conditioning than with logic. All major disasters throughout the 1970s killed over 142,000 people a year on average. Yet each year some 15 million children die of malnutrition-related causes, and nowhere is this carnage described as a disaster.
>
> (Wijkman and Timberlake, *Natural Disasters*)

CHAPTER TWELVE

HONDURAS: WHOSE EARTH?

'It's *God's* earth', was the answer intended to resound amongst creation-conscious Christians at the end of Tear Fund's 'Whose Earth?' youth action initiative produced in conjunction with the major Christian festival, Spring Harvest, in 1992.

In fact Tear Fund has been quietly green long before it became fashionable. Many British supporters were paying to plant trees in places they had hardly heard of years before the rest of the population started taking their hangovers to the bottle bank.

Another difference is that Tear Fund has been *naturally* green; conserving God's creation was an obvious part of enabling people to thrive in their own habitat. Development is about planting trees, not stripping the forest bare.

'Plant a tree for 20p' was a Tear Fund slogan in 1977. George Hoffman had visited Haiti in the Caribbean, the poorest country in the western hemisphere. It was also the scene of 'the first national ecological disaster in the western hemisphere'.

Natural disaster, prolonged drought and widespread deforestation combined with political corruption had led to the average Haitian receiving only two-thirds of the food he needed for a normal diet. No less than two million people – more than one-third of the entire population – faced the prospect of starvation.

Trapped in the poverty syndrome, the vast majority of rural peasants had been forced into the primitive form of 'slash and burn' agricultural survival which had 'literally murdered the land'.

Forests had been cut for fire and charcoal. Slopes had been burned for planting food crops. Livestock had been forced to graze in areas unsuitable for pasture. In 20 years, forested land had shrunk from 80 per cent to 9 per cent of the island, half of which was second-growth scrub. And the death of the forest had triggered unchecked soil erosion so that only one-third of the land was suitable for cultivation.

To restore some of this land to a potentially workable condition, Tear Fund, in association with the Cooperative Evangelique d'Haiti, undertook to finance the planting of 100,000 trees annually for the following five years. To purchase, nurture and cultivate one tree for five years cost just 20p, little more than the price of a Mars bar in those days.

Tear Fund supporters had already responded generously to an

appeal for Haiti in Christmas 1976, enabling more than £24,000 to be allocated to community development projects there. Now they responded again to this harvest appeal, and the greening of a tiny island began.

Fighting for the forest

In 1990, Tear Fund supporters were again at the forefront of green development. This time they had to get involved in green politics – lobbying the President of Honduras on behalf of the Indian peoples of his land, viewed by many in Honduras as second-class citizens.

The battleground was Mosquitia, the popular name for a section of the Atlantic coast area in Honduras and neighbouring Nicaragua. Its unique combination of rainforest, grassy plains, rivers and lagoons was cut off from the rest of the country by mountains and dense jungle, and it could only be reached by sea or air.

Although the Indians had lived in Mosquitia for centuries, they had few legal rights to their land. As a result they could easily be forced off by those invading their territory – and there were plenty of potential invaders. Cattle-ranchers, peasant farmers and business interests were moving into Mosquitia to exploit the natural resources of timber, oil and gold; tens of thousands of hectares of rainforest had already been cleared. At that rate of destruction, the jungle would disappear in just ten years.

To protect their lifestyle and environment, the Indians' leaders were lobbying the Honduran government of President Callejas

Small-scale, church-based holistic development offers the best route for expressing a Christian concern for the whole of God's creation. The aim is sustainable programmes that protect and enhance the environment as they meet the needs of the poor.

The demand for fuel by a growing population puts great strain on the forestry resources of Two Thirds World countries. Tear Fund is involved in imaginative reforestation programmes in many of these countries, providing for immediate needs and restoring the environment.

for land titles. They were supported by MOPAWI, a Christian development agency aiming to help the Indian communities survive the massive economic and social changes affecting their traditional homeland. (MOPAWI's name is an abbreviation of the Miskito Indian words for 'development of the Mosquitia').

Tear Times readers picked up their pens and, following a model letter set out for them, earnestly encouraged *Excelentisimo Senor Presidente* in the steps he had already taken to prevent commercial exploitation of the rainforest. They also sent copies of their letters to the Honduran ambassador in London.

No one can tell what reaction the Honduran President may have had when informed of the deluge of letters from Britain, as well as communication of the British people's concern from his man in London, but this pressure and pressure within his own country won some time for the Indians.

The immediate result was that his government overturned a potentially disastrous logging agreement signed with Stone Container Corporation, a US multi national. Within Honduras, churches, businesses, unions and the media attacked the prospect of Stone being handed exclusive rights to one million hectares of Mosquitia's pine forest for 40 years.

Although a cause for celebration, the Indians' problems were not over. Other companies threatened the future of Mosquitia, and Tear Fund environmentalist Andrew Leake urged supporters to remember that a battle had been won, but the war was far from over.

Andrew and Maria Leake

Before leaving the UK in February 1989 with her husband Andrew to start a four-year assignment in Honduras, Maria Leake had to learn how to make radio programmes. While Andrew was an environmentalist, Maria's post involved co-ordinating radio programmes and producing publicity material for local people, including the untrained Miskito Indian lobster divers who were exploited by ship-owners and suffered ill-effects from their diving. Maria found her course gave her the confidence to tackle making a programme; as a teacher, she planned to make it educational!

As Communication and Development Co-ordinators, Andrew and Maria joined other Tear Fund personnel at Puerto Lempira, Honduras, to work with Christian group MOPAWI.

Sent in to help the Indians protect what land they had for their own economic future as well as for the rainforest, Andrew and Maria found themselves living amongst the Indians who lived in small villages, taking fruits from the forest, fish from the rivers and such delicacies as iguana eggs and armadilloes. Their houses are roofed with a natural palm which lasts about 30 years. Their presence in the rainforest had made little impact, as they lived in harmony with their surroundings. 'All that stands to be lost if the forest-clearing continues eastwards,' says Andrew.

No roads led into the region until 1992, when a road was cut through the forest near the Indians' villages to transport lumber. Andrew and Maria initially had to raise the Indians' awareness of the threat to their lifestyle – they had no newspapers or television. So with Tear Fund support they took the Indians up-river to demonstrate the effects of deforestation and introduced them to government officials, as well as liaising with the officials on behalf of the Indians. Andrew claims to have made some significant advances in helping the Indians become aware of their legal position, sadly a weak one, so they can influence the authorities themselves. A major breakthrough came with the production of a map showing the Indians use of the land; now there was a scientific basis for discussion about the most suitable development of the area.

Maria specialised in making the Indians' situation known to the rest of Honduras by enabling groups of Indians to publicise their case in the press; she travelled all round the country in the process.

Between 1986 and 1992, more than £370,000 was given for the Mosquitia Indians' community development work. MOPAWI's development projects included agriculture, land rights, media, education, women in development, credit, health and marketing.

Whose Earth?

Meanwhile, over three thousand people, the majority teenagers, 'Joined the World in Hyde Park' on September 5th 1992. Organised by Youth for Christ and Tear Fund, the event was the climax of the launch period of this youth initiative which aimed to give a focus for evangelical concern for the environment.

Over 650 groups had registered to be part of the project, which not only provides teaching resources but also hosts of practical ideas for action, from cleaning up beaches to digging ponds.

Thousands of signatures were delivered to the Prime Minister just before he left for the Earth Summit in Rio, while at Hyde Park, television cameras perched in a helicopter recorded the scene as the largest ever people map of the world was created below. Youth for Christ are continuing to work with Tear Fund to communicate this simple meassage: 'Whose Earth? God's Earth!'

CHAPTER THIRTEEN

TEARCRAFT: A WORLD OF CREATION

'Not a hand-out, but a hand up'
'Not just aid, but trade'
'Not just nice presents bought from a glossy catalogue, but a vital source of desperately needed employment and human dignity'

Ian Prior and Richard Adams had been at college together. Ian was working at Tear Fund in 1974, and Richard was attempting to establish a company importing goods on a fair basis from the Third World. In 1974 Peter McNee, a New Zealand missionary in Bangladesh, was looking for a way to help desperately needy women by selling their jute handicrafts. He spoke to Ian Prior at Tear Fund who put him in touch with Richard Adams. The result was a £1,000 order of goods, and a mail order leaflet listing eleven items.

Then came another phone call from Tear Fund. A plane packed with blankets, powdered milk and basic medical supplies was due to leave for Bangladesh in two weeks time. Would Richard like to make good use of the return flight and fill it with handicrafts? So one week later he was visiting eager producers, delighted to have an opportunity to sell their goods in the midst of disaster.

The VC10 returned to Stanstead airport, and rapid plans were prepared to warehouse and then sell the crafts. The result was that two days before Christmas 1974 Tearcraft was registered as a business name, and its first catalogue went out in February 1975. The craft was stored in Newcastle-upon-Tyne, and the business expanded rapidly. But by 1979 growing disagreements about exactly how the company should be run resulted in Richard Adams leaving and establishing Traidcraft, while Tear Fund continued with Tearcraft marketing goods made by groups that were linked with evangelical Christians who saw the handicraft production process as an outworking of the mission of the church.

Each year a colourful catalogue is produced and people all over Britain and Ireland have the opportunity to buy quality hand-made products from many different countries around the world. When they do so, they are enabling people to have the dignity to earn their own living, providing jobs and income to people who often have no alternative. The work has the added advantage of often bringing additional income to women, who can exercise their creative skills in their domestic situation.

Tearcraft – a catalogue of social action

Tearcraft has come a long way since the first consignment of handicrafts arrived in 1974. By 1991 it had sold £9 million worth of goods and had a turnover of £1 million.

The woven table mats gracing a British dining table brought hope and often food to a family who might have faced hunger, because Tearcraft has provided employment for tens of thousands of men and women throughout the Third World.

Dozens of Christian-run craft groups in many countries have been able to train and provide employment for people without any other paid work. And whether in the Himalayas of Nepal or the desert plains of Peru, each group is also committed to preaching the gospel of Jesus Christ as an integral part of their mission.

Job creation

The ability to provide for oneself and for dependants through dignified and fulfilling work is an important aspect of life for people made in the image of God. Tear Fund supports projects which provide resources for the creation of productive and properly rewarded jobs.

Training

Investment in developing individual skills and gifts is vital for the well-being of the church and community. Tear Fund's Partners in Training scheme provides practical training of young people, whether in nursing, agriculture, carpentry or tailoring. In turn their skills may find their way into the Tearcraft catalogue.

For Aida Tomo of the Philippines, handicrafts are not a hobby, but the means by which her family eats properly. She lives near her work in a squatter area known as 'Corazon de Jesus' – 'Heart of Jesus'. The house is down little alleys, the sun almost blocked out, with no sanitation or privacy. Yet her work has brought her family small luxuries, like a television, and she attends a Bible study group with ten of her neighbours, having become a Christian here.

The gospel has not only brought some material comfort and security into her life, but also, she claims, a contentment with what she has.

Christmas comes to Thailand

Carefully painted miniature reindeer and angels made of jute are some of the wooden Christmas decorations made by Lao Song Handicrafts in Thailand.

In 1966 the Lao Song people were close to starvation, until the Church of Christ provided sewing machines, patterns and materials. Today Lao Song Handicrafts has hundreds of craftsmen and women in several villages receiving a vital supplement to their income from farming.

Lao Song Handicrafts aims to help anyone in need, Christian or not. Yet many have become Christians and a church has been established as individuals have discovered something of God's great love for them.

Going into all the world from Gospel House

When John Karunaratne became a Christian, his life changed; he gave up his job and became an evangelist. But unemployment is high in Sri Lanka, so John began a craft business to train and employ young men. Tear Fund financed a building – Gospel House – completed in 1979.

One of the people to receive help was Gerry Fernando, a full-time evangelist. In turn, Gerry has been able to buy land, build a home, and give work to local young people. Tearcraft saw the potential of his work and put in large orders.

Many of the young men employed at Gospel House have become Christians. They in turn visit surrounding villages, overcoming opposition to tell others about Jesus. John Karumaratne died, but Gospel House Handicrafts continues as a vital and productive reminder of his vision and commitment, now run by his wife and sons.

'No choices'

No choices, silent voices cry out to me.
No choices, these voices won't let me be.

These words were the haunting refrain of a song written by Christian rock musician Martyn Joseph after visiting Thailand in 1988.

While visiting a number of Tear Fund-supported projects, his experiences and reactions were filmed for a video appropriately entitled *No Choices*.

During the time he spent in Bangkok, the nation's capital, his senses were bombarded by a host of contrasts, from the splendour of gold-leafed temples to the squalor of filthy slum dwellings; from the sweet smell of incense coming from the wayside shrines, to the choking stench of the putrid open sewers alongside many homes.

He saw evidence of the lack of choice facing many young people in Thailand in the bars and brothels of the city, where girls and boys are sold into prostitution out of economic necessity. In the McKean Rehabilitation Institute he met leprosy patients whose choices were limited by the crippling effects of withered limbs and deformity. Elsewhere he saw how poverty, deprivation and injustice reduce people's choices and leave them without hope.

The memories that would stay with him were of 'these wonderful people who have so much grace in their lives' – the people who had come alongside those who suffer, meeting their needs and giving them choices for the future.

Rehabilitation

There have been some beautiful examples of the gospel being good news for the whole person at the McKean Rehabilitation Institute in Chiang Mai, Thailand. Founded in 1908 by James McKean, a doctor and missionary, it has encouraged people who once suffered from leprosy to develop new skills, which in turn gives them greater confidence in their abilities and their worth as human beings made in God's image.

Heather Smith, an Australian working at McKean said, 'There's a need to minister to the whole person; psychologically and spiritually as well as physically, especially when the sufferer has been rejected by society and feels guilt. Many need to find love, acceptance, and a reason for living – and many have found it through Jesus.'

At McKean, a handicraft programme for children extended to training several young women and then young men, who needed to support themselves and gain a sense of achievement at the same

time. Spatter painting was the answer; it required care rather than artistic skill, and the resulting greetings cards were not only attractive, but saleable. They still feature in the Tearcraft catalogue.

The first time that Heather Smith was able to report the sale of the spatter painted cards to the young men, they did not believe her. They looked at her and said, 'You don't mean someone bought what we made?'

When Heather reassured them that that was precisely what she meant, the men straightened up: 'I saw them put their shoulders back and smile – they were so proud . . .'

Another beneficiary of the McKean treatment was Rabiap, a girl who developed leprosy as a teenager.

> When I was at school I had a pain in my elbow, when I moved it. In my village we believed that spirits probably caused things that were wrong and so we looked for treatment against the spirits. My father died when I was very little and my mother had to go out and look for work to make a living for us.

A missionary brought Rabiap to the McKean Rehabilitation Institute where she was housed in a dormitory and continued her schooling while receiving operations so she could use her hands again.

Once she was able to start making handicrafts with her restored hands, Rabiap experienced another change in her life:

> My personality was that I was cross a lot and I liked to complain and fuss . . . Then I received the experience that God can give

us, to know him. This experience I just never want to forget and I thank God that he was given me a new life. I will never go back to the old sort of life that I had. He is teaching me to be patient . . . First I thought, why did God allow me to be like this, then I came to thank God that I am like this, because I have come to know the fullness of his love here.

Tear Fund supporters first met Rabiap in *Man of Compassion*. When Martyn Joseph visited McKean he met her too, and discovered that she was now married to another patient at McKean, and the proud mother of a tiny baby. Martyn, whose own baby had just been born, was particularly moved by the poignant sight of love being given and received so warmly by someone who had been thrown on the scrapheap.

A man of potential

Wong Wiang has been more blessed than many other leprosy sufferers, whose disease often results in social ostracism.

Twenty-nine years ago he went for treatment to the McKean Rehabilitation Institute. After nine years, he was not only cured but had learnt practical craft skills. He had also found faith in Christ.

But the care and practical support he received from McKean did not end there. In 1978 Wong Wiang began his own business to support his wife and three sons with a loan from McKean. Today his greatest concern is finding markets for his jewellery and finely-painted lacquerware.

Helping him with design ideas has been Rose Collins, a Tear Fund craft consultant. Although he markets his goods through Tearcraft and SEL, the French equivalent of Tear Fund, direct selling is still hindered by prejudice when local people see his disfigured hands and avoid him, fearful of contracting leprosy themselves. Nonetheless, the business employs 12 workers and Wong Wiang is keen to expand. With the help of his friends and McKean and Rose's advice, the work of his hands has given Wong Wiang a new lease of life.

CHAPTER FOURTEEN
WOMEN LIKE US

Among the very poor, women are often the poorest.
A United Nations report concluded that women make up half the world's population and one-third of the official workforce – yet they own less than 1 per cent of the world's property and receive only 10 per cent of its income.

So it is not surprising that women are the main users of aid. To them falls the responsibility of child care and domestic health, with many having to grow as well as cook their family's food – in some parts of Africa, women grow as much as 80 per cent of the population's food.

Traditional culture and customs often militate against a proper intake of food. In 1984, Tear Fund worker Muriel Scott, who ran a community health programme in Parbatipur, Bangladesh, described how tribeswomen in her area were brought up to believe that the initial breast milk was bad for their babies. Instead they were fed on rice and barley water for the first few days of their life. During the first week after giving birth, the mother would eat only rice and salt, with no vegetables, fruit, eggs or meat, as these were considered harmful. If the child got diarrhoea he received no fluids or food at all. Muriel's conclusion: 'Many of the illnesses are associated with strong food taboos which usually involve the patient eating only rice and salt or rice water.'

In 1993, women are still bearing the physical strain. Childbearing is made all the more wearing because women are often undernourished before they become pregnant. Lack of money, information or access to facilities means that complications in pregnancy or birth are often endured rather than dealt with, often resulting in more serious ill health or death for both mother and child.

These are the traditional patterns of life which have been passed down through the centuries. Yet as modernised farming methods have been adopted and cities have spread in the Third World, women have frequently lost out. Their husbands are drawn into the cities to work, often through necessity, leaving their wives with the entire burden of caring for the family day to day.

Where small, self-sufficient farms have been taken over by large cash crop plantations, women have often become an underpaid workforce on other people's land instead of growing food for their families on their own plot. As literacy becomes more and more important, many women are left out of decision making or denied their rights in the workplace because they are unable to read or write.

Teaching

Ruth Nickerson, a trained teacher of handicapped children from Huntingdon, Cambridgeshire, began a four-year assignment as a literacy teacher at the Ban Vinai Refugee Camp in Thailand in 1984, home to refugees from all over South-east Asia, including the Vietnamese boat people. Many at Ban Vinai had belonged to the anti-Communist resistance in Laos and had been forced to flee when the Communists took control of their country. Ruth's work also featured in the Tear Fund video, *Man of Compassion*, and a beautifully produced book based on her drawings, poems and diary entitled *Promise of Dawn*.

Thailand was not new to Ruth: she had already spent three years there at a Christian health clinic for refugees at Maejarim. In a 'functionally built' bamboo and thatch schoolroom, she and her two colleagues launched their own 'primary education system' for many of the children and teenagers in the camp. This was in addition to her main task, setting up a woman's literacy programme for South-East Asian Outreach. Her responsibilities included training teachers, supervising the design and preparation of teaching materials and writing new material for literacy development.

> I felt it very important to teach a group of women from scratch, those who'd never been to school, some who couldn't hold a pencil – and then I could really understand the ladies' difficulties and how I could help them. I really enjoy the hours I spend in the classroom every day and I create new materials depending on their needs.

Ruth's teaching also gave her many opportunities to share the women's lives and get to know their families. 'I'm able to laugh and cry with them and just love them with the love of Christ.'

Once she was challenged to pray for a sick man in the camp hospital to be healed. His family had performed pagan spirit ceremonies; now it was Jesus' turn. Although Ruth prayed with some uncertainty, nonetheless the man started to recover.

That was a more dramatic example of compassion. At places like Ban Vinai, people like Ruth are challenged every day to be like Jesus, 'not to feel compassion, but to *act* it', as George Hoffman said. As Ruth said, clenching her fists as she did so, 'Compassion isn't a sweet and sentimental feeling at all – sometimes it's just raw anger.'

Women like us

Not all Third World women are downtrodden. There are plenty of shining examples of women who have been given the confidence to improve their own and others' situations. Tear Fund has been privileged to support their initiative and contribute to their spiritual impact on their areas.

One of these is Florence Yeboah, leader of a dynamic ministry to the women of Ghana. GHACOE, born at the Ghana Congress on Evangelisation in 1977 when women delegates met together to pray for their nation, now has over 60 groups – 4,500 members in ten regions of the country.

Florence has seen that God is a God of power and change, something which is often accepted more easily in Africa, which has a greater consciousness of spiritual forces.

Florence has seen the gospel improving women's lives in several ways. Firstly women are regularly prayed with for healing and deliverance from evil spirits as part of GHACOE's evangelistic crusades. 'We want them to put their confidence in Jesus Christ,' says Florence. 'They see that he is real, and a friend who stays closer than a brother.'

As well as being the founder of GHACOE, Florence is a coun-
sellor for RURCON, an Africa-based network of Christian rural
counsellors. In keeping with her concern for development, women
in GHACOE groups have the opportunity to learn practical skills:
cooking, sewing and making batik – all helpful in boosting the family
income. GHACOE has also started to set up a demonstration farm
to teach women how to grow basic foods like cassava, and a small
cassava-processing factory provides training for them, as well as
generating income to support the wider ministry.

Recognising the powerful combination of dynamic evangelism and
development in Florence's ministry, Tear Fund stepped in to help
GHACOE arrange an exchange visit with women from Namirembe
Diocese, Uganda, for Florence to share her skills and experience.
Women from GHACOE groups often take a leading role in their
own fellowships, setting an example to others.

How the other half lives

Tear Fund's 1987 video, *Women Like Us*, was in many ways an
eye-opener. By juxtaposing British women's largely uninformed and
clichéd opinions about Third World conditions with three women's
lives in Ecuador, it provided embarrassing evidence that in some
respects those with the most knew as little as those with the least. It
also proved that women have common concerns, no matter how great
their affluence; in the film the women worried about their children's
health, were keen for them to do well at school and beyond, found it
hard to make ends meet, tried to keep their homes clean and sought
the companionship of other women.

Esilda Quinteros had lived in
Guayaquil, Ecuador, for 14 years.
She had been deserted by two
husbands and the cameras found
her bringing up six children and
two grandchildren on her own.
From a part-time job washing
clothes she earned the equivalent of £1.10 a day, less 20 pence
for a bus ride across the city
to her work.

Her home was near a river which regularly overflows in winter
and floods the house, inducing diarrhoea or fever in her children,
for whom she cannot afford medicine. Through Tear Fund, one of
her daughters had been enabled to have a proper education.

Maria Morscho had seven children aged from three months
to 13 years old. Her husband
only earned the equivalent of
£8 a week, so she did part-time
washing and ironing. When she
went out of the house she would
padlock the door and give the
key to the children, telling them
to call the neighbours if anyone
broke in. She hoped that a good
education through Tear Fund's
Childcare scheme would enable
her children to break out of the
poverty cycle which trapped her
and her husband.

Lourdes Ochoa Sanchez had seen
three of her eight children die,
including her only daughter at
one year old. Bad health had
affected two of her sons, one
of whom was at school thanks
to support by a group of retired
people in Britain. The kerosene
stove she used was a real fire
hazard. Clean water only arrives

every few days on a tanker, and she had to pay about 20 pence to
have her oil drum filled.

Her husband sold clothes and cosmetics on the street. On a
good day they had enough money for breakfast and lunch. If he
had made a little more they could buy enough food for a small
evening meal.

Women Like Us made no attempt to hide the poverty in which
these women lived, but by showing British women's reactions it
showed that material possessions cannot hide spiritual poverty.

Waging war for women

Tear Fund recognises the vital contribution made by women to
community development and sees them as a priority. As their
health, education and economic status improves, so families and
communities will become stronger. Instead of a cycle of poverty, a
chain of development can be set into motion from which women, men
and children will all benefit.

For these reasons Tear Fund supports evangelical Christian

partners who are working to improve the social, economic and spiritual well-being of women.

Planting for life

How do you get round a superstition popular in parts of west Kenya which maintains that a woman who plants a tree is causing her husband's death? This was one of the challenges facing Dr Roger Sharland, a Tear Fund worker who directs the RDE (Rural Development by Extension) department of the Organisation of African Independent Churches.

The solution? You get women to plant *miti ya mama*, women's trees, which can be used for firewood rather than the eucalyptus or cypress traditionally planted by men.

Working largely through women's church fellowship groups, the RDE field workers have been able to discuss craft work, agricultural practices and such technology as energy saving stoves. As women put development principles into practice as a group, their confidence grows.

And the trees? If all the church women decide to plant trees, no one suffers the isolation of being different from the rest!

Meanwhile the RDE hopes their methods will be discussed in churches throughout Africa.

Growing old
In rich countries, men can expect to live to 68 and women to 76. In poor countries, life expectancy is 54 for men and 56 for women.

Health
An African woman is 200 times more likely to die in childbirth than her European counterpart.

Just under half the women in developing countries outside China are estimated to be anaemic.

Families
Over half the population growth in the 1990s will be in Africa and South Asia. (United Nations Family Planning Agency)

Education
Three-quarters of women aged 25 and over are still illiterate in much of Africa and Asia.

Education makes you healthy

When the prophet Hosea pronounced, 'My people perish for lack of knowledge', he could have been talking of women's conditions.

Over and over again Dr Bachan of the busy Harriet Benson

Memorial Hospital in Uttar Pradesh province, India, sees the health problems caused by lack of knowledge.

In 1992 the hospital, in association with the Family Planning Foundation, launched a community development programme which will eventually cover 11 villages. By focussing initially on health education and literacy, the programme should combat poverty and ignorance, encouraging people to seek treatment for minor illnesses rather than ignore them because of transport difficulties, lack of money and cultural taboos.

Traditionally, children are not given solid food until they have a number of teeth, a practice which can cause serious growth problems. Dr Bachan is determined his health workers will deal with these and other issues and at the same time give people the opportunity to hear the gospel that inspires all the work of the Harriet Benson Memorial Hospital.

If he improves women's literacy – and he hopes to raise women's literacy rate in the hospital's catchment area from 4 per cent to 40 per cent – then more women will be able to read. It has been documented that children of women who can read are in far better health and rarely die. The hospital also employs 'Bible women' to share the gospel with women, because it is not acceptable for women to gather together with men to hear male evangelists when they come to villages. In many villages the Bible women have visited, Dr Bachan reports that 'the women were very happy. They said, "No one ever talked to us. Can someone love me? Can God love me?"'

'If you educate a man you educate an individual, but if you educate a woman, you educate a nation.'
Agri, a Ghanaian philosopher

A day in the life of a Nepali mum

Devi's mum rises well before dawn, about 4.30 a.m. As always, the first task is to spread a fresh layer of mud, dung and water over the floor of the house. No time to stop, there is a buffalo to milk, firewood to chop, the fire to light, the baby to nurse. Then to grind grain in order to make chapati type bread.

With the family feeling content after their tea and bread, Devi's mum begins on the next round of jobs. This involves three trips to the spring to carry water, trying to persuade Devi and Siami (aged six) to help her with cutting and carrying food for the buffalo and feeding the pig and chickens.

Next, she washes some clothes, sweeps the house and sharpens the knife. In between she tries also to attend to the needs of Leela (aged three) and Ek Bahadur (aged one). By then it is time to cook the first main meal of the day, usually eaten about 10.00 a.m. As usual it is rice and curried vegetables and today a kind of bean stew as a treat. After washing the pots and pans comes the best part of the day, a few minutes of sitting and chatting with other village women. Not for long, however. Today Devi's mum has to carry buffalo dung to their fields. This involves several trips up and down steep paths carrying the load in a straw basket supported by a band around her forehead. So Devi stays to look after Ek Bahadur and Leela.

By 4.00 p.m. it is time to stop work in the fields and continue the round of chores at home, chopping more firewood, re-lighting the fire in order to cook more tea and chapatis. Then a couple more trips to carry water, the animals to feed, the buffalo to milk, etc. Next, Devi's mum grinds some corn and makes porridge for supper.

By now it is dark. After the children are settled and asleep, she sits by the fire making rope from grasses that she has previously cut, soaked and dried. As she does so she thinks about tomorrow when they are going to the temple to sacrifice a chicken and offer *puja* (worship) to the gods. She hopes the baby's cough will then begin to get better, he seems so thin and cries so much. If only there was more time to look after him . . .

Written to illustrate the daily reality of life in Nepal.

CHAPTER FIFTEEN

WALK IN HIS SHOES

'Prayer sustained nurse held by Sudanese rebels,' ran a *Daily Telegraph* headline on 28th August 1987.

For seven weeks, Tear Fund nurse Heather Sinclair, 29, and three American teachers, were the subject of prayers from Christians all over Britain and Ireland, including the Archbishop of Canterbury.

It all began at midnight on 6th July when four men claiming to be from the Sudanese People's Liberation Army (SPLA) arrived in Heather's bedroom and ordered her to get ready to leave. Heather had sufficient courage to order them to leave her room while she dressed, then she and the others, two men and a woman, were marched away. Over the next seven weeks they marched 200 miles, sleeping rough and never knowing if they would be released.

Yet Heather did not fear for her life, because the SPLA told them that they were being evacuated for their own safety and would be given back to their own people.

The kidnappers, some of them teenagers and armed with rifles, had left a note back at the base, so Tear Fund and Heather's family were soon alerted to the situation.

The knowledge that thousands at home would be praying for them provided emotional support for Heather and the others. She had come to Sudan just four months previously from Draperstown, Co Londonderry, in order to help provide basic medical treatment and training for mothers and children in an area seriously affected by drought and conflict.

During the long march, they prayed every day and read the Bible. 'We knew we had God's power and protection. When a few of us got sick, we worried whether we would get the right medicine, but again the Lord was good – the days we were resting were the days we were most ill.

Finally they were released at the Kenyan border, and after a press conference Heather was flown home to an emotional reunion with her parents.

Asked today about the long-term effects of that abduction, Heather says, 'I didn't feel much need for counselling afterwards, because they had reassured us that we were being evacuated for our own safety. I certainly didn't feel my life was in danger as, say, Terry

Waite must have felt. And as a team of four Christians we were able to share our emotions.'

On her return, Heather made a reassessment of her life, and remained convinced that God was calling her back overseas. Just one year after Sudan, she spent a year in Swaziland as a nurse on a community health project, followed by two years working with Cambodian refugees in Thailand. She plans to return to Africa with Tear Fund before the end of 1993, once again to work with the national church in a community health role.

'The Sudan experience was the greatest preparation possible for working with refugees,' she says. 'When you're kidnapped, you leave everything behind, everything that identifies your particular way of life.'

Her lasting memory is of God's faithfulness. 'Sometimes I still cling to that – I know that God called me to Sudan and had prepared a path for me.'

Tear Fund workers are well prepared for overseas service, and happily Heather Sinclair's experience is an exception.

Over the past 25 years, hundreds of men and women have travelled to share their skills, both in performing tasks and training others. To begin with it was often for just a few months; now it is for four-year assignments, with many returning to similar tasks for second or third terms. In recent years the Graduate Apprenticeship Programme has also seen many young people working overseas for one year as they test their suitability for a longer-term commitment, as have Task Force Teams, for shorter periods of time.

Rebuilding lives

Tear Fund only started recruiting its own personnel in 1973, a year when millions in India and Ethiopia faced starvation from drought. A new staff member, Ian Prior, was drafted in to set up the Overseas Personnel Department. Immediately he started arranging for doctors, nurses, builders, agriculturalists and engineers to get straight to trouble spots, where they could use their skills to save lives both short and long-term.

Overseas workers are well aware that they do not have a job for

life with Tear Fund. They are there to make themselves redundant, having trained local workers in their particular area of expertise. One of the intentions of the overseas personnel programme is to pass on skills to others who have not had the opportunities to learn.'

Workers are selected who have a clear Christian commitment and flexibility to fit in with overseas partners.

People are not sent out to work for Tear Fund, but for partners, so they need to understand the partner's ethos. What do *they* want to learn – what is *their* vision for this particular task?

Many people find, however, that they are learning just as much as those they have been sent to teach. They enter a new world with new ways of thinking and doing things. Serving in Haiti, Cathy discovered that the Haitians were people-orientated rather than time-orientated.

> I initially got very upset by interruptions to my plan for the day, when I couldn't achieve the goals I'd set for myself. That's a Western mind-set, whereas what makes the Haitians' day is if you visit them, sit down with them and talk and listen. They share the little they have with such generosity.

In a strange culture, the Western mind frequently has to adjust its expectations; what are their host country's values? Who makes the decisions in a community – do the old or the young take the lead? How do men and women relate to each other in public? Where do children fit into society?

All this is vital knowledge for the overseas worker: 'The important thing is to understand the people you're serving and working with,' says Cathy.

> Understanding their world means listening and making yourself vulnerable, being open to not knowing, which means in turn that however many qualifications and however much experience you have for working in the West, you have to admit you do not necessarily know how you'll do your job or how you'll be able to communicate. You may find you can say 'Good morning' and nothing else! Or you buy what looks like bananas and they're cooking, not eating, bananas!

Thus the most successful overseas workers learn how to be taught themselves, right from the beginning of their service, and they often learn the hard way.

So people from Britain and Ireland wanting to serve overseas have to be carefully selected, although it is amazing how often the right person turns up, aware of God's prompting, to fit a particular need.

To meet all the requirements of their partners and the jobs themselves, Tear Fund seek to work with the potential overseas worker's home church, expecting it to have provided the basic Christian discipleship necessary for anyone moving overseas to pass on their professional abilities. Tear Fund have devised a preparation and equipping process – a training cycle to encourage personal, spiritual and professional development at significant stages in the lives of those committed to the Lord Jesus Christ and in his name to cross-cultural ministry among the poor.

In other words, Tear Fund recognises the truth of the popular quote, 'The body can be transported to another part of the world in a matter of hours, but it may take years for the soul to catch up.'

Potential workers may find they are recommended to take more time to deepen their roots in the Lord before going overseas, or to spend a little more time gaining specialist knowledge about their area of service: an agriculturalist may be sent back to university for a week of guided reading about aspects of forestry in Nepal, or a mechanic sent on a course to learn the intricacies of particular makes of vehicle.

After selection and any extra 'equipping' for the task in hand, workers take a two-week orientation course, where they examine the biblical basis of mission and such questions as:

What about other faiths?

How do I share *my* faith overseas?

What do we mean by development?

Other topics cover more immediate needs: personal health and hygiene, spiritual warfare and inter-personal relationships overseas . . .

Recent graduates going overseas with GAP (Graduate Apprenticeship Programme) simply take the two week orientation course; their year is intended to give them a flavour of overseas service and help them decide if this is the life for them.

Those on the Task-Force Teams, who travel in a small group to work on a particular project for just six weeks, have been required sometimes to take part in Tear Fund's own simulated overseas experience; a night in the Essex forest with a mock-up airport and new language. They had to find their way from one area to another, cope with an accident, sleep rough, make a shelter, buy provisions and watch a turkey being killed . . . Their reactions are not recorded, but the work of task-force teams has been very effective in recent years, diverse as Mozambique and Russia.

It is easy to 'dry up' spiritually overseas, so Tear Fund encourages churches and friends not only to send sermons and inspirational messages on cassette but also plenty of newsy letters. A prayer partner keeps everyone informed of their welfare and latest news.

Workers are also likely to have at least one Tear Fund visitor during their four years overseas.

Sue Mills worked overseas with Tear Fund in a variety of places facing the desperate famine situation in Ethiopia in 1974; caring for children evacuated from Vietnam; working with Nicaraguan refugees in Honduras and village communities in Pakistan. She describes four stages in people's attitudes during their first year overseas.

- There's the tourist stage, enthusiasm tinged with hesitancy, when everything's new.
- Then there's the frustration stage, when homesickness and tiredness make it harder to cope with the cultural adjustments being asked of you in communication, thought patterns, attitudes and food.
- Thirdly comes the most critical stage, when you could slide downhill, asking yourself if Tear Fund really know what they're doing!
- Lastly, comes a period of reflection and re-thinking. You're settled down and recognise the worth of those differences you've challenged before, realising they work in that particular setting.

At some point during these stages comes a reckoning with God. Suddenly the workers become aware that God has brought them overseas for his own reasons. These may be in part to improve their technical abilities, but also to make them dependent on him and help them discover aspects of their personality that he wants to change, all of which could only be accomplished by detaching the person from their friends and familiar surroundings.

In the early days there was an almost equal number of single and married overseas personnel; nowadays most overseas workers are married. Generally it is the husband who is recruited to a job, which can leave some wives wondering what role they will play overseas. Tear Fund explores the options for the other partner and tries to find an outlet for any special training or gift he or she may have.

With these roles to be worked out, both husbands, wives and single people away from their families for a prolonged period welcome the two-month break after two years. At this point Tear Fund takes a practical and spiritual health check to see what is needed. Currently being developed is a training module on relief and development work to help give workers new ideas to tackle work problems overseas. It is also hoped to bring together people who have finished a period of service overseas to unwind together; only other overseas workers or those with some experience of Third World work can understand their particular joys and frustrations as they seek to come back to earth and ask themselves such questions as, 'Who am I? Where am I going from here? What's been happening in Britain while I've been away?'

Such fundamental questions, however, only underline the scale of change encountered by those who willingly offer themselves for overseas service and are prepared to pay the price in personal and professional terms.

People used to ask Bill Latham, formerly Deputy Director of Tear Fund, 'Was it very depressing?' when I returned from an overseas trip. But I always came back inspired and encouraged by the amazing commitment of the Christians who were working out there. In Chad, on my first trip, a missionary doctor just exuded concern and love for people. In other places, worse than that, the Christians were always doing such a magnificent job. When I went to the north of Kenya, a remote, ugly part of the world which was just volcanic rock, I couldn't wait for my three days to be up. I asked a nurse who was there for three years how she actually stuck it for that length of time, and she said, 'When God wants you in a place, anywhere becomes beautiful'.

Kevin McKemey, who served with Tear Fund in Argentina from 1970–1982 says

> Over the years we have most valued the spiritual basis of Tear Fund's ministry. Of course, we have appreciated the extent of financial support received and the relationship of trust which has grown between us, a fact which is evident in the response to requests and the positive encouragement that we have received.
>
> But more importantly we have appreciated the prayer backing and concern from Christians and churches linked with Tear Fund. I personally believe that this is one of the most valuable assets Tear Fund has, and my hope is that bureaucracy will never invade Tear Fund to the loss of the inter-personal links with those supporting the organisation and the people it is supporting through its variety of programmes.

Personnel

Overseas workers can still make a vital contribution to holistic development. Tear Fund supports around 100 in more than 25 countries – usually for assignments of four years. They go overseas at the request of Tear Fund's Christian partners, and work in healthcare, agriculture, rehabilitation projects, water supply and sanitation, forestry, administration, training – and much more. Training national personnel is an integral part of their work.

Alastair and Sheila Taylor work at Ringili Demonstration Farm, a practical training centre for agricultural and other development subjects, under the auspices of the Church of Uganda in Arua. They are both graduates of Reading University and have one son, Nathaniel, 2. Alastair is seen here demonstrating practical soil conservation, while Sheila demonstrates soya cookery. Apart from missing family, friends and the chip shop, they enjoy 'seeing ideas that we demonstrate being taken up by people and, of course, the joy of helping people to come to know Christ in a real way.'

'It took a five-day trip to do half a day's work,' says design engineer Jeremy Thake, holder of an MSc in Agricultural Engineering and an MA (Oxon) in Engineering Science. The work was reassembling a microhydro turbine at Ghandruk in Nepal, just south of Amapwna. Jeremy is working in microhydro power at Butwal, Nepal, where he brought his wife and three children under 10.

With Jeremy is Fiona Stratton, who came onto the Graduate Apprenticeship Programme with a first in Mechanical Engineering. When her year in Nepal is over, Fiona is looking forward to being 'able to go into a room, safe in the knowledge that it isn't infested by rats and lizards!'

CHAPTER SIXTEEN
TEAR FUND TODAY

The mail van arrives bright and early. Five or six sacks every day for 100 Church Road, Teddington. An imposing yellow-bricked building with some newly planted ivy starting to climb the walls. The mail sacks are taken up to the top floor to be opened – opening the post is almost a full-time job. Four or five hundred letters a day, some with cheques, some with questions, some from overseas partners, some from school children.

If a gift is involved it's important to deal with it quickly and efficiently. Cash and cheques are taken to the bank every day, but increasingly people give regularly via direct debit and standing orders. So bank statements have to be checked carefully, and all donations logged against the right name on the computer, so that acknowledgements can be sent and the records kept accurate.

The computer is crucial to all Tear Fund's administration. It holds the names and addresses of all supporters; it records donations; it keeps track of funds; it ensures accurate payments go to overseas partners and personnel; it produces letters, charts, memos – all sorts of information. It also needs special care and attention, programming, training, troubleshooting.

All this is what people sometimes call 'overheads'. But senior staff at Tear Fund object to this term, because, they say, it implies something people would rather do without, when the truth is finance and administration are vital parts in the whole work of Tear Fund, vital to both giver and overseas partner. Nonetheless, they realise that costs in this area need to be monitored and controlled. The target is to keep these administrative costs below 7 per cent of Tear Fund's income, at the same time aiming to be as efficient as possible in the use of these resources.

Children's letters are given special attention. 'Children often give with tremendous generosity and enthusiasm,' says Stephen Rand, 'and we want to make sure they know it is appreciated.' They can receive a letter from Terry Tearaway, a cartoon character who appears in his own magazine three times a year. He was invented some years ago to help children identify with the situations he was able to describe as Tear Fund's Special Investigator. He has now been joined by his sister Tina, and their adventures, in magazine cartoons and on video, have proved very popular with primary age children.

Children's letters are important in another way in Graham Fairbairn's Home Department. Partners in Childcare is just one of the programmes overseen here, and it includes the possibility of the supporter receiving an occasional letter from the child who is being assisted through their regular donations of £13 per month. The letters all come into the department and are sent out to the appropriate supporter by a small team of volunteers who come in each Thursday for this particular task.

All the partnership schemes are designed to help give people a focus for their prayers and giving. There is a recognition that for many people the world is just too big to take on in its entirety, but broken down into more accurate pieces information can be absorbed and involvement encouraged and maintained.

This is clearly very important to the Home Department and the whole of Tear Fund. In all their contacts with individual supporters, there is the aim of encouragement, of attempting to be responsive to people's enthusiasm. The Enquiry Unit receives many telephone calls with a wide range of requests, many centring on information about how gifts can be channelled to particular people or programmes.

For many people, their enthusiasm has been channelled into giving up time for Tear Fund. There is an army of voluntary representatives, about 500, who tell others about Tear Fund, sell Tearcraft goods, show videos, arrange displays and run prayer groups. In addition there are over 2,000 church representatives, who act as a bridge for information to pass from Tear Fund to their church. A great deal of effort is taken to ensure that all these volunteers are informed and kept up-to-date.

The Co-ordinators, Tear Fund's regional staff, are vital to that process. There are nine of them – six in England, one in Wales, Ireland and Scotland. They encourage volunteers, speak in churches and help to keep the organisation in touch with the grass roots of support.

All this personal contact with supporters is backed up by an enormous range of published material. Videos, slide sets, OHP packs, simulation games and posters for churches; Tear Times, leaflets and booklets for individuals. A lot of work goes into prayer information for both groups. Tear Fund recently launched World Watch Prayer Link to give a service of regular monthly prayer sheets covering world events for individual and group use. Church service material is very popular and very important. Poems, sketches, prayers, sermon notes, children's talks – all these reflect the commitment to working with and through local churches in Britain and Ireland.

Tear Fund staff conference 1992

The Communications Department are responsible for all the information that goes out from 100 Church Road. The aim is threefold,
explains Stephen Rand:

> We want to communicate something of what the Bible says
> about God's concern for the poor, and something about the
> reality of life in the Third World, both good and bad. Then
> Tear Fund can be seen as a channel that allows Christians to
> respond to biblical teaching on the basis of understanding and
> information. That's why we don't organise fun-raising events
> in the traditional sense, or door-to-door collections. We want
> God's people to make an informed, committed response, to see
> their involvement with Tear Fund as an outworking of their
> Christian discipleship.

All these resources are stored in the building and sent out by the
Resources Section. At Tear Fund Sunday, Harvest and Christmas,
they are particularly busy; on each occasion about 1,000 churches
use some resources to help them think about the needs of the poor.
Sales of the video *Compassion has the Heart*, featuring Cliff Richard,
have passed 3,500.

The information that is used by the Communications Department
is dependent on the elaborate network of partners built up by the
Overseas Department over 25 years. Because Tear Fund enables
other evangelical Christians around the world to act in the face of

need, the home office staff in the Overseas Department are vital to the effectiveness of all that is done.

The regional desks – Latin America, Southern and Eastern Africa, West and Central Africa, Asia, Europe and the Middle East – are the focus for building relationships with partner groups and handling their specific requests for financial support. Detailed budgets and proposals come in from over 80 countries; they are carefully assessed by both staff and external advisors and consultants, many of whom give their time and expertise on a voluntary basis; final funding decisions are overseen by a board committee, so that accountability is maintained, and decisions are in line with agreed criteria. Often there will be careful consultation with partners, as both they and Tear Fund are concerned to ensure that the best possible work is done in the name of Christ.

This has led to the growth of the Partner Support of the Overseas Department. Increasingly partners are looking for expertise, advice, sometimes a sounding board for ideas. Tear Fund is aware that a partner in one country may well have gained experience that would help a partner in another. So staff may be based in Teddington, but their focus is on the overseas work and their time is spent in arranging training workshops, sharing experiences, offering advice where requested. *Footsteps* is a magazine produced in four languages, designed to give very practical information for development workers, the great majority of whom will be nationals working in their own country.

One vital area for partner support is when disaster strikes. Mike Wall is responsible for the Disaster Response Unit, and training has become an important part of his work. 'There is much that can be done before a disaster comes,' he explains. 'It is people who are vulnerable that suffer in a disaster, and some of that vulnerability can be recognised and removed – after all, prevention is better than cure.' Mike has helped to produce a Training Manual called Christian Perspectives on Disaster Management, and this has already been used to train individual Christians, equipping them with skills that can ultimately save lives.

But when disaster does come and relief is needed urgently, Tear Fund is geared to respond. One of the wonders of the modern banking system is just how quickly funds can be transferred, enabling Christians on the spot to obtain the supplies that are most urgently needed.

Funds are important, but people rank high on Tear Fund's list of priorities. The Personnel Department not only deals with the overseas workers, those on the Graduate Apprenticeship Programme and the short-term teams programme; it also looks after Tear Fund's 170 home staff, making appointments, ensuring salaries are paid, and all the other tasks that are required. Visitors to the Tear Fund office are often surprised by the size of the whole operation but staff are convinced they are equally often able to leave impressed with the scope of the work and the professionalism with which it is approached. An Open Day held in 1992 prompted so many positive reactions from those that came, that there is now a permanent invitation for supporters to ring and make an appointment to come and see for themselves the reality of Tear Fund today.

Communicating the vision

The education of Christians in the churches of Britain and Ireland is an integral part of Tear Fund's ministry; relating biblical teaching to the realities of life for the poor; developing understanding of the causes of poverty; and encouraging an appropriate response from young and old in prayer and giving.

One obvious reason for Tear Fund's rapid growth is its confident use of modern media. Beginning with dramatic posters, it progressed to its newspaper, *Tear Times*, to soundstrips and, in the mid-1970s, to videos.

Over the years, a series of people have been responsible for communicating the vision. Some have worked on these various resources; others have visited churches and groups all over the country, being seen as a personal representative of the work of Tear Fund.

Margaret Winfield – educating for understanding

Many people who have become involved with Tear Fund can trace this back to contact with Margaret. As Education Secretary in the 70s she travelled thousands of miles to talk to students, often in very small goups, sharing her enthusiasm for a Christian concern for the poor.

She worked on church resource materials, wrote detailed letters in response to enquiries, and was an effective speaker to informal groups and in the pulpit. She is now married to Rev Vic Filer, and maintains her involvement with Tear Fund as a voluntary representative.

Bill Latham – sharing the vision

'He's 31, Single. He lives in north London. In April he joins the staff of Tear Fund as Education Officer.'

In such terms *Tear Times* tantalised its supporters in early 1970. Bill had worked as a journalist and RE teacher, but his attributes went beyond a keen news sense and local church commitment. One of Bill's close friends was fellow Crusader leader Cliff Richard, for whom he organised speaking engagements. Bill knew little of Tear Fund before receiving an invitation from George Hoffman to join him and two others and develop Tear Fund.

His flair with young people was to be exploited in talks to youth clubs, but it was soon apparent to him that the job was much wider. He began putting together slide sequences, all the rage at the time, consisting of 30 slides and a script, ideal for showing in darkened church halls.

Dewi Hughes – theology and conviction

Dewi is another who became involved as a result of Tear Fund's voluntary representatives scheme. A Welshman who communicates in English as his second language, he left his post as Lecturer in Theology at the Polytechnic of Wales to become Tear Fund's first Welsh Coordinator.

In 1993 he took on a new role for the whole of the UK and Ireland as Theological Education Advisor. The main focus of the post is to liaise with theological and Bible colleges to encourage a greater awareness of holistic mission in general and Tear Fund in particular. This means that he has also been enabled to take on a public role as a speaker on Tear Fund's behalf, and a more private role encouraging theological reflection within the organisation.

Tony Neeves – advertising through persuasion

As the eyes, or lens, through which many had Tear Fund's ministry brought home to them, Tony visited over 30 countries in 20 years.

He joined Tear Fund after working for it in his 'spare time' – every evening and weekend! Formerly art director of a leading London advertising agency, he was committed to advertising through persuasion rather than shocking hardened public into giving.

As an experienced advertising professional, Tony was able to advise Tear Fund in an area which other Christian organisations frequently eschewed.

He explained how to identify the target audience – a young one, previously untapped – and to define the message they were to receive. 'We had to convey the message that Christ loves the poor and commands us in the Bible to love and help the poor also, to step alongside them – and we ignore this at our peril.'

The younger audience was excited by the whole approach, according to Tony, because they were shown that 'giving is a two-way process'. They were not being asked to throw money at the problem of the poor in the developing world, but, by means of regular information, to become involved in prayer and the education of others within their churches. In turn they felt rewarded, which produced a 'very committed support base'.

Stephen Rand – expanding the vision

Currently Communications Director, Stephen, like Bill Latham, came out of secondary teaching to educate a wider public.

Before joining Tear Fund in 1979, he was a history teacher at a boys' comprehensive school in Croydon. His first role at Tear Fund was developing the network of voluntary area representatives, backed up by full-time area co-ordinators. After initiating Tear Fund's church representatives scheme, Stephen moved on to become Director of the Education Service department, responsible for youth, student and adult education.

He soon became involved in producing a series of videos, making the most of the new technology available to get Tear Fund's message into homes across the country. As Communications Director he is responsible for that overall message, and over the years he has travelled the country, speaking widely in churches, student groups and events such as Spring Harvest and Greenbelt, as well as organising Tear Fund's major towns such as *Broken Image* and *The Road to Freedom*.

Graham Fairbairn – encouraging support

Currently Home Director, Graham is responsible for all the
communication at an individual
level to supporters, particularly
those involved as voluntary representatives and in the various
partnership programmes. His involvement began as a voluntary
representative in his home town
of Ballymena in Northern Ireland, while working in industry
there. In 1979 he was appointed
as Co-ordinator for Ireland, becoming a well-known face in
churches in Ireland as he travelled to encourage supporters
who were often very enthusiastic
and committed. He was particularly delighted when the Pres-
byterian Church officially recognised Tear Fund as one of the

development agencies they would support as a denomination.

His move to the senior team at Teddington meant that his role
was effectively extended to the whole of the country, combining
responsibility for many important administrative sections of Tear
Fund with a continuing role as a speaker and communicator.

CHAPTER SEVENTEEN

GOD'S LOVE IN ACTION

by David Adeney, Executive Director

Inevitably this book can be no more than a series of snapshots, impressions of the complex and exciting work of Tear Fund over 25 years. In a sense, God is the only one who knows the full story, and he is the one who takes the ultimate credit for anything and everything positive that has been achieved through Tear Fund.

Those of us who have worked for Tear Fund know that we have been part of the exciting reawakening of evangelical social concern that has taken place since the 1960s, and we dare to believe that Tear Fund has itself contributed to that process, as well as clearly growing as a result of it.

While recognising the evidence of God's blessing and acknowledging our dependence on his Spirit it is right to recognise the original vision of Morgan Derham and those who initially established Tear Fund. That vision was, of course, taken up and developed by George Hoffman, who established the basic principles of so much of Tear Fund's activities, not least the vital importance of clear and effective communication. George was skilled in his straightforward exposition of the Bible and a powerful storyteller, bringing the world in all its horror and its hope to the attention of evangelical Christians, whether through an article, a sermon or even a flimsy vinyl record. In this way the vision became a reality.

The world has certainly changed since 1968. Charities are often accused of emphasising negatives in order to encourage response, so let us recognise the positive achievements of recent years. Infant mortality has been reduced in many countries; more children are able to go to school; world food production has increased. In fact, there are sufficient encouragements for the goal of material improvement to be sufficiently realistic to pursue. We need not, and can not, despair – we must continue to mobilise resources, seek the political will and the collective determination to move on. For the Christian this determination springs from a vision of the world as God intended it to be and also in obedience to God's demands to care for the poor, so clearly revealed in the Bible.

This determination gave birth to Tear Fund, and continues to motivate us as we face the future. Our commitment, reaffirmed recently in the Purpose and Mission Statement, is to remain faithful to the principles that were established in the beginning, but also to be flexible in our response to the challenges that lie ahead. The key to success in any Christian venture is the combination of a solid foundation in biblical principles with a dynamic response to the guidance of the Holy Spirit.

As we face the future, we believe there are three key factors that will shape the development of Tear Fund.

Increasing need

We are forced to the conclusion that despite all the hopeful signs of progress, human need will increase. There will be growing demands for assistance from Tear Fund. The continuing growth of world population means not only that there are more mouths to feed, but that the concentration of population growth in the world's poorest countries and cities adds particular stresses and strains in those areas least able to cope. The key to this problem lies in both development through the creation of opportunities for economic growth and child spacing through birth control. Increasing wealth in a family and community seems to lead to smaller families, rather than the other way round. This raises deep and fundamental issues of wealth and power, women's rights, the rights of the unborn, and not least our view of God's activity in the future. Tear Fund is actively seeking to listen to our partners and to develop a biblical response to these issues: we see this as a major challenge to Christian thought and action. Perhaps the most significant aspect of this challenge is to seek justice for the poor, rather than expecting the poor to continue to pay the price for maintaining the privileges of the wealthy.

There will also be more specific challenges to be faced. It is impossible to escape the conclusion that war, drought and debt will lead to continuing demands for relief from various areas in Africa. The encouraging response to drought in Southern Africa in 1992 has to be balanced against the ongoing agony of Sudan and Somalia.

The dreadful conflict in former Yugoslavia is indicative of the

vulnerability of the whole of the former Communist bloc to fragmen-
tation, ethnic conflict and economic collapse. Freedom has brought
more opportunities for the church to serve, but it has also brought
a complex of threats to stability and a potential for suffering on a
massive scale.

In Africa particularly and in the rest of the world, scientists
attempt to follow the march of the AIDS epidemic and calculate
its impact. Even the most optimistic scenario leads to severe conclusions – not only in terms of individual suffering and death, but
also for the families and communities that remain. The Christian
community that teaches and lives by God's standards of sexual
behaviour, is in a unique position to respond to this challenge.

A growing Church

The Christian Community is growing. What could be a greater
encouragement in the face of increasing human need? It is growing
in numbers: it is growing in maturity; it is growing in its ability to
respond effectively to the needs of those around it and within it.

It has been Tear Fund's enormous privilege to work with and
through Christians around the world. In the beginning they were
often expatriate missionaries; now, overwhelmingly, Tear Fund
works with national Christians and local church groups sensitive
to their own culture, rooted in their communities and increasingly
equipped to respond effectively. In many areas of the world, in Africa

particularly, the church is often the most effective local community organisation. Tear Fund's commitment to working through the church or christian organisations in order to ensure that everyone has the opportunity to hear of Jesus Christ as part of the help they receive, is both practical and effective.

So as the church grows and develops it will be in a position to do more and more in response to the increasing needs on its doorstep; it will be looking for support in terms of prayer, skill-sharing and finance; ultimately, it will be looking for a growing expression of fellowship in the body of Christ. Tear Fund is not so much about transferring resources from North to South, but more about developing a genuine sharing between members of the same family.

Resources available

We have been humbled by the generosity of God's people over 25 years. No one imagined that an evangelical charity could grow in this way. Despite economic gloom, genuine recession and increasing alternatives for spending, more and more people have given more and more money. There is a recognition of the needs and an expression of confidence in Tear Fund. We believe this will continue, so increasing the resources that we receive to make available to our partners around the world. Others may talk of 'compassion fatigue', but that is no option for Christians. Recent developments in evangelism in Britain encourage us to believe that the link between obedience to God and concern for others will be strengthened in very practical ways.

Increasing resources do bring greater responsibility. One of the encouragements of recent months here in the office has been greater efficiency at transferring those resources quickly to our partners. We now have only the equivalent three or four weeks income in the bank. Those who support Tear Fund can be confident that needs will always be met quickly and effectively. Their gifts are used where they are needed, not in building up reserves and investments, but

in expressing the love of God through Christians in over 80 countries around the world.

At the same time we have been developing our ability to be of greater service to our overseas partners, not only offering financial resources, but advice, training, evaluation and encouragement. Tear Fund is at an exciting phase of its development, with more high quality staff joining the team to help increase our partners effectiveness in bringing good news to the poor.

Here at home we are also putting a greater emphasis on our prayer resources and helping inform our supporters and encourage them to speak and act on behalf of the poor. This is, we believe, a dynamic and biblical balance that promotes the broadest possible response to the challenge of a world in need. It is the challenge for us all to be effective channels of God's love in action.

David Adeney
Executive Director

Tear Fund's Purpose and Mission Statement:
The purpose of Tear Fund is to serve Jesus Christ by enabling those who share evangelical Christian beliefs to bring good news to the poor.

- Proclaiming and demonstrating the gospel for the whole person through support of Christian relief and development.

- Working through a world-wide network of evangelical Christian partners.

- Encouraging partnership in prayer and support from Christians in Britain and Ireland.

- Seeking at all times to be obedient to biblical teaching.

For further information please write to:

Tear Fund
100 Church Road
Teddington
Middx TW11 8QE

Communities

Jeanne Hinton

Photographs by Christopher Phillips

The stories and spirituality of twelve European communities

Iona (Scotland), Post Green, Lee Abbey, Little Gidding, Stepney
Friary, Darvell Bruderhof (all in England), Corrymeela (Northern
Ireland), Ekklesia (Holland), L'Arche (France), Grandchamp
(Switzerland), St Egidio (Italy) and OCJ (Germany) are all
flourishing Christian communities today.

* What makes each distinctive?
* How does each fulfil its role in society?
* How does each live apart from the world – yet in the
  world?
* How does living together really work out?

Discover the heart of each community, the people who work and
worship in each, the reasons they exist – and flourish today, a
thousand years after the height of monasticism.

Let Jeanne Hinton's text and Christopher Phillips' photographs
lead you on their pilgrimage, as they share a moment of the life of
these communities.